A Field Guide To Flight

REVISED EDITION

On The Aviation Trail In Dayton, Ohio

by Mary Ann Johnson

LANDFALL PRESS
DAYTON, OHIO
1996

PHOTOGRAPH SOURCES

Carillon Park 58; Centerville city 78; Dayton Airshow, by Paul Kusy 76; Dayton International Airport 129; Dayton-Montgomery County Public Library 46, 53, 55, 64, 83, 100 top, 104, 110, 111, 113; John Jameson 27; Rich Johnson 91; Kettering-Moraine Museum 65, 66; Marlin W.Todd 18; United States Air Force Museum 89; Wright-Patterson Air Force Base 102; Wright State University Archives and Special Collections 16, 19, 20, 21, 22, 23, 24, 28, 30, 33, 36, 37, 39, 40, 41, 44, 48, 49, 52, 59, 62, 63, 67, 68, 69, 72, 74, 80, 81, 82, 93, 96, 98, 99, 100 bottom, 105, 107, 115, 119, 121, 124, 132, 133.

Maps by Frank Pauer

Cover photograph: Orville, left, and Wilbur Wright with the Flyer II at their Huffman Prairie flying field in 1904 (Wright State University Archives and Special Collections).

For information address Landfall Press, Inc., 5171 Chapin St., Dayton, Ohio 45429.

ISBN 0-913428-58-2

Library of Congress No. 85-082342

AVIATION TRAIL, INC.

All profits from *A Field Guide to Flight: On the Aviation Trail in Dayton, Ohio* go to Aviation Trail, Inc., a nonprofit corporation formed in 1981 to preserve and promote the Dayton area's unique aviation heritage.

Aviation Trail, Inc. developed the Aviation Trail described in this book and owns one of the sites: the Aviation Trail Museum and Visitors Center (WA 1). It also provided the initial preservation efforts for the two buildings now owned by the National Park Service: The Wright Cycle Company (WA 3) and the Hoover Block (WA 2).

Aviation Trail, Inc., P. 0. Box 633, Wright Brothers Branch, Dayton, Ohio 45409

ACKNOWLEDGEMENTS

I thoroughly enjoyed researching and writing *A Field Guide To Flight: On The Aviation Trail in Dayton, Ohio*, but the project would have been impossible without the support and assistance of many others, to whom I extend my appreciation.

Especially supportive was the Aviation Trail, Inc. Board of Trustees, who first envisioned a "trail" of Dayton area aviation-related sites and selected those described in this book. Also especially supportive was my husband, Rich, who enthusiastically accompanied me on repeated visits to the sites and provided support in many other ways.

Others provided valuable assistance by commenting on all or part of early drafts, including Ed Hamlyn, Patrick Nolan, John Dussault, Lois Walker, Patrick Foltz, Dick Baughman, Roz Young, Lieutenant Colonel Allan V Cummings, Charles L. Fister and Bill Ford, who also suggested the title and helped arrange the book's publication.

Also, I am indebted to the many people who provided information or directed me to information sources. Among these are J. H. Meyer, M.D., Harold Johnson, Terry Miller, Hank Cates, Melba Hunt, Darryl Kenning, Wayne Watkins, Frederick I. Kuhns, Susan Marks, Marlin Todd, Captain Gus Elliott, Karen L. McDaniel, Kevin Smith, Ruth Scott, Doris Scott, Robert Nadolsky, Bill Buckles, Don Reed, Jim Reedy, Mary Aldridge and John G. Lepp.

And I would like to give special recognition to Jerry Sharkey, who first proposed the Aviation Trail concept at a conference of community leaders in November 1980.

To all of you -- many, many thanks.

Mary Ann Johnson, 1986

ADDITIONAL ACKNOWLEDGEMENTS

I would like to thank the many individuals who helped with this revised edition of *A Field Guide to Flight: On the Aviation Trail in Dayton, Ohio* by offering comments or providing updated or new information about individual sites.

Among them are Aviation Trail Trustees George J. Wedekind, Jr., John F. Darst, James Custer, Roger McClure, Fred C. Fisk and Harold Johnson and Aviation Trail Advisors Wilkinson Wright, Gus Brunsman, Helen A. Kavanaugh, Bill Gibson, Mary Mathews and Don Pabst.

Others include Robert Petersen, Richard Martin, Nancy Horlacher, Ed Ruff, Brian Hackett, Dennis Nolan, Richard A. Ball, Jr., Melba Hunt, John Warlick, Jenna Kimberlin, Toni Walder, Shari E. Christy, Jan Ferguson, David Duell, Dawne Dewey, Dorothy Smith, Arthur R. Disbrow, Naomi and Maynard Brackney, Nelson Borchers, Roy Williams and Wayne Watkins.

And a special thanks to my husband, Rich Johnson, who accompanied me on my visits to each of the sites.

I appreciate very much the assistance and support of each of you.

Mary Ann Johnson, 1996

PREFACE TO THE REVISED EDITION

I have come to think of this 1996 revised edition of *A Field Guide to Flight: On the Aviation Trail in Dayton, Ohio* as the Centennial Edition because it was just 100 years ago, in August 1896, that Wilbur and Orville Wright began their search to unlock the secrets of powered flight -- a search that began here in Dayton, Ohio.

The story of that search and its successful conclusion in 1903, as well as the substantial local aviation history that followed, was covered in the 1986 edition through profiles of 45 aviation-related sites. In the intervening ten years, some of those sites were lost or relocated and new ones added; thus, the current Aviation Trail now totals 47 sites. A review of these changes shows:

- The Dayton Convention and Exhibition Center was deleted from the Central Loop when a remodeling project eliminated the *First Flight Mural* in the lobby and the National Aviation Hall of Fame portraits along the walls of the mezzanine.
- The Aviation Trail Museum and Visitors Center, now under construction, was added to the West Anchor.
- The new Wright B Flyer hangar at the Dayton-Wright Brothers Airport was added to the South Loop.
- The new WACO Aircraft Museum in Troy was added to the North Loop.
- The International Women's Air and Space Museum abandoned its proposed site at Dayton International Airport in favor of a museum in the restored Asahel Wright House in Centerville, which already was a South Loop site based on its association with the Wright brothers' great-uncle.
- And the National Aviation Hall of Fame broke ground for its new museum, which will be a separate structure attached to the United States Air Force Museum, already an East Anchor site.

Other revisions to the 1986 edition include updated information about the exhibits, open hours and fees charged, as well as changes and expansions and/or updating of a number of the site profiles themselves. An example of the latter is Wright-Patterson Air Force Base, on the East Anchor, which has undergone major organizational changes.

Nevertheless, in spite of the revisions, the basic story of the Dayton area's unique aviation history remains the same, starting with the invention of the airplane by Wilbur and Orville Wright up to the aerospace projects of the future now under development at Wright-Patterson Air Force Base.

Mary Ann Johnson, August 1996

CONTENTS

INTRODUCTION

This book is a carefully researched and detailed catalog of events and places that have always been part of the fabric of my life; some of them in actual experience, others by family associations. During their early years in Dayton the Wright family lived on the West Side, along Third Street west of the Miami River. My grandfather, Lorin, lived at 7 Hawthorn Street with his father Milton, his brothers Wilbur and Orville and his sister Katharine. His older brother Reuchlin had married and established his own home. When Lorin married Ivonette Stokes in January 1892, he moved to 117 South Horace Street, just a few blocks east. My father Milton was born there in November of that year.

My Aunt Ivy (Ivonette) was born at the Horace Street home in 1896, Aunt Lonnie (Leontine) in 1898 and Uncle Bus (Horace) in 1901. Lorin moved his family briefly to Plant Street in Riverdale in 1902 but returned to live at 1243 West Second Street in May 1903. This home was just one block north, through the alley, from 1127 West Third Street where Orville and Wilbur had moved their bicycle shop in 1897. There in the spring of 1903 the brothers were building and gathering in the workroom at the back of the shop the parts needed to assemble the world's first successful flying machine. While I have never lived on the West Side, I have heard the family stories about those days so often that I feel as though I had lived there.

When my grandmother had errands to run she often left one or more of her children at the bicycle shop or at the Hawthorn Street home to be watched by their willing uncles. Aunt Ivy was known to get into mischief sometimes so her uncles solved that problem with their usual ingenuity by putting her on top of the icebox. The icebox was high enough that Aunt Ivy could be counted to stay there out of mischief, at least temporarily.

Uncle Bus caused this historic note to be entered in his grandfather's diary:

In the evening we had a time with Horace, who resented being sent up to our house. He said, "I want to go home!" I finally subdued him.

Many years later my father could still vividly recall the smell of spruce shavings in the bicycle shop where his uncles worked on spars and struts for their planes and gliders. I have a picture of him as a teenager, dressed in a suit, standing proudly in front of their West Side home. On the table in front of him is a large model of a Wright Flyer, one of many that he built to sell to Dayton citizens after his uncles had returned home, now internationally famous, in 1909. In 1911, Aunt Ivy, Aunt Lonnie and their cousin Ellwyn (Reuchlin's daughter) took the Green Line streetcar downtown from the West Side and rode the traction out to Simms Station where their Uncle Orv took them each for an airplane ride.

In later years I visited the West Side from time to time, usually with my grandfather, to go to Uncle Orv's laboratory on North Broadway. My brother Milton and I, and often our cousin Jack Miller, prowled around the big workshop while the men talked. Then Uncle Orv might show us the latest project he was working on, always something interesting. I can remember an automatic transmission and a code typewriter and especially a mechanical phonograph record changer that was a story all in itself.

Lorin and Orville remained very close all their lives, visiting one another almost daily, my grandfather stopping by the laboratory on his way home to lunch, or Uncle Orv dropping into Lorin's home on Grand Avenue or his toy factory on Front Street before going back to his laboratory.

There were many family gatherings at Hawthorn Hill, Uncle Orv's beautiful, rather formal mansion on Harman Avenue in Oakwood. The big center hall, running the full depth of the home, was an ideal place for children to play. There was a Chinese box on the hall table where Uncle Orv and Aunt Katharine put their pennies, to be distributed when children visited. And there was a drawer in one corner of the breakfast room that was full of toys. Uncle Orv particularly liked German mechanical toys: a little man who stroked a pool cue to push a miniature billiard ball into the corner pocket, a clown who balanced a spinning ball on his nose and a monkey that rode on a motorcycle.

Thanksgiving and Christmas Eve dinners were always at Hawthorn Hill. Uncle Orv carved the turkey while his housekeeper, Carrie Grumbach, served the other delicious, hearty dishes. The menu varied some, but there was always turkey, mashed potatoes (which Uncle Orv and Uncle Bus dearly loved) and a molded pear salad with pimento cheese and a sweet homemade dressing. Dessert was homemade, too.

At Christmas, hand-turned ice cream was packed in two big watermelon molds and then brought to the table on a platter garnished with red and green maraschino cherries. It was always chocolate ice cream on the outside and fig ice cream on the inside, accompanied by angel food cake flavored with almond. Even with these desserts, Uncle Orv's sweet tooth was still not satisfied. When the demitasse was served, he spooned sugar into the little cup until it was almost ready to overflow.

This book, then, is a very special volume for me because it recalls these and many other memories of places and events in Dayton and around the Miami Valley. But even without these personal associations, the book gives an impressive account of remarkable happenings.

Around the turn of the century Dayton was a ferment of inventive genius, scientific research and boundless energy that has since grown and spread to change the course of world history. I thank the members of Aviation Trail who have identified and marked these historic footprints left across the Miami Valley as its people pushed forward to set the world in flight.

Wilkinson Wright
September 30, 1985

CHRONOLOGY

1796   April 1: The first settlers arrive in Dayton after an 11-day boat trip up the Great Miami River from Cincinnati, Ohio. Wilbur and Orville Wright's great-great-grandmother, Catharine Van Cleve Thompson, is the first woman ashore.

1867   April 16: Wilbur Wright is born near Millville, Indiana to Catharine's great-grandson, Milton Wright, and his wife, Susan.

1869   Spring: The Milton Wright family arrives in Dayton for their first stay. They leave in June 1878 and return permanently in June 1884.

1871   August 19: Orville Wright is born at 7 Hawthorn Street, the Wright home in Dayton.

1896   Wilbur and Orville Wright begin their search for the secrets of human flight after reading about Otto Lilienthal's glider experiments in Germany.

1899   Summer: The Wright brothers develop their wing-warping theory of lateral control after studying the flight of birds at Pinnacle Hill, south of Dayton, starting in 1897.

1900   October: The Wrights test their wing-warping theory on a man-carrying glider at Kitty Hawk, North Carolina.

1901   Fall: The Wrights test their second glider at Kitty Hawk. It is the largest glider ever flown up to that time.

1902   September 19 - October 24: The Wrights test their third glider at Kitty Hawk. The tests prove the brothers have a controllable man-carrying machine needing only the addition of propellers and an engine to achieve powered flight.

1903   December 17: Orville Wright makes the world's first man-carrying, controllable powered flight at Kitty Hawk. The machine, the Flyer I, is damaged after the fourth flight of the day and never flown again.

1904   May 26 - December 9: The Wrights test their Flyer II at Huffman Prairie, their flying field east of Dayton.

1905   June 23 - October 16: The Wrights test their Flyer III at Huffman Prairie. The Flyer III is the world's first practical airplane.

1906   May 22: The first Wright patent application is granted. The application had been filed March 23, 1903.

1908   August 8: Wilbur makes the first European flight in a Wright machine, at Le Mans, France.

1909   August 2: The world's first purchase of a military airplane, a Wright Model A, is approved by General James Allen, Chief Signal Officer, United States Army.
November 22: Wilbur and Orville Wright form The Wright Company to manufacture their invention.

1910   May 10: The Wrights open their first permanent flying school, at Huffman Prairie. The school is closed in 1916.
June 13: The Wright exhibition flying team gives its first exhibition, at Indianapolis, Indiana. The team is disbanded in November 1911.
June 29: The Wright Company produces the first Model B, the world's first mass-produced airplane.
November 7: Wright Company pilot Phil O. Parmalee, flying a Model B, makes the world's first commercial flight, from Huffman Prairie to Columbus, Ohio.

1912   May 30: Wilbur Wright dies in Dayton at the age of 45.

1914   April 28: Orville Wright, his sister, Katharine, and his father, Milton, move to *Hawthorn Hill*, the Wright mansion in the

Dayton suburb of Oakwood. Orville will live there until his death in 1948.

1915   October 15: Orville Wright sells The Wright Company. In 1916 the company merges with the Glenn L. Martin Company to form the Wright-Martin Aircraft Company.

1916   November: Orville moves into his laboratory at 15 North Broadway Street, which he occupies until his death in 1948.

1917   Hartzell Walnut Propeller Company is formed in Piqua, Ohio to manufacture airplane propellers for World War I. The company is now called Hartzell Propeller Inc.
April 11: Charles F. Kettering and Edward A. Deeds form the Dayton Wright Airplane Company to manufacture airplanes for World War I. Orville Wright is a director. The company is acquired by General Motors Corporation in 1919.
May: Wilbur Wright Field is established to conduct firearms tests and to train pilots for World War I. The field includes the Wrights' former Huffman Prairie flying field.
June: The Fairfield Aviation General Supply Depot is formed to supply Signal Corps aviation schools in the eastern United States for World War I.
October: McCook Field is formed to centralize the country's aviation research activities in support of the United States war effort.

1919   April 28: Leslie Irvin makes the first jump with a modern freefall parachute, at McCook Field.

1922   October 20: McCook test pilot Lieutenant Harold R. Harris makes the first emergency jump with a freefall parachute, landing in a grape arbor in the backyard of a house on Troy Street.

1923   Weaver Aircraft Company opens a factory in Troy, Ohio. Later known as the Waco Aircraft Company, it becomes the largest United States producer of civil aircraft in the 1920s and 1930s.
May 2 - 3: McCook test pilots Lieutenants John A. Macready and Oakley G. Kelly make the first nonstop flight across the continent.

1924   April 6 - September 28: McCook is the logistics center for the first flight around the world and three of McCook's personnel take part in the flight.

1927   October 12: Wright Field is dedicated. The field, located east of Dayton, is built as a replacement for McCook Field after McCook outgrows its cramped space near downtown Dayton.

1928   A group of Dayton businessmen open a private airport in Vandalia. The field becomes the Dayton Municipal Airport in 1936.

1931   July 6: Patterson Field is established on land that includes the former Wilbur Wright Field and Fairfield Aviation General Supply Depot.

1935   McCauley Aviation Corporation is formed to manufacture airplane propellers by Ernest G. McCauley, a former Wright Field engineer. The company becomes a division of Cessna Aircraft Company in 1960.

1936   Lear Avia, Inc., owned by William P. Lear, who will later develop the Learjet, opens a factory in Vandalia to manufacture aircraft instruments. The company moves to Piqua in 1941, then to Michigan in 1946.

1940   Aeroproducts Division of General Motors Corporation is established to manufacture Aeroprop propellers for World War II. The division is absorbed by the GM Allison Division, Indianapolis, Indiana in 1961.

1948   January 13: Wright-Patterson Air Force Base is formed through the merger of Wright Field and Patterson Field after a separate air service, the United States Air Force, is established on July 26, 1947.

1969   July 20: Neil Armstrong, of Wapakoneta, Ohio, is the first human to set foot on the moon.

ON THE AVIATION TRAIL

Wilbur and Orville Wright built the world's first successful airplane in 1903 in Dayton, Ohio, making Dayton the birthplace of aviation. But Dayton is more than the birthplace of aviation, it is also the cradle of aviation and the incubator of aerospace adventures yet to come.

Through the device of a series of profiles about the sites on Dayton's Aviation Trail, *A Field Guide To Flight* tells the story of Dayton's unique place in aviation history and her continuing role as a center of aerospace research and development. Along the Trail you will:

- Meet some of the local early balloonists,
- Explore the neighborhood where Wilbur and Orville Wright lived and worked and learn the details of how they invented and perfected the airplane, including their early flying experiments at Huffman Prairie,
- Follow the development of military aviation from the establishment of McCook Field in World War I as the nation's first military aviation research and development center up to the present day research and development work at Wright-Patterson Air Force Base,
- Learn the history of the local aviation industry, including the stories of the Dayton Wright Airplane Company, manufacturer of the DeHaviland-4, the only all American-produced airplane to see action in World War I, and of the Waco Aircraft Company, the country's leading manufacturer of civil aircraft during the period between the two World Wars,
- Meet some of the early pilots, such as the test pilots at McCook Field who risked their lives in adventures like the first nonstop flight across the continent and the first flight around the world,
- Learn about the first commercial airplane flight, the first emergency freefall parachute jump and other "firsts" that took place in Dayton,
- And learn the locations of Dayton's rich store of aviation artifacts and memorabilia, including the original Wright Flyer III at Carillon Historical Park, the Wright Brothers Collection in the archives of Wright State University and the collection of military aircraft at the United States Air Force Museum.

The Dayton Aviation Trail as described in *A Field Guide to Flight* is organized as a self-guided tour to be taken in person or from your armchair. The 47 sites are divided geographically into five segments: the West Anchor (WA), followed by the Central Loop (CL), in downtown Dayton, and the South Loop (SL), East Anchor (EA) and North Loop (NL). However, the Trail is designed so that visitors (or readers) can begin at any one of the sites, depending upon interest or convenience.

For those of you following the Trail in person, each site is identified by a blue and white sign with the Aviation Trail logo (the Wright Flyer I). And you can record your visit on the Aviation Trail log at the end of this book.

So, bon voyage as you follow the Aviation Trail in Dayton, Ohio, the birthplace of aviation.

1. Aviation Trail Museum and Visitors Center

2. Hoover Block

3. The Wright Cycle Company

4. Wright Family Home Site

5. First Wright Brothers Printing Shop Site

6. Orville Wright's Laboratory Site

7. Last Wright Brothers Bicycle Shop Site

8. First Wright Brothers Bicycle Shop Site

9. Second Wright Brothers Bicycle Shop Site

10. First Wright Company Factory Site

11. Former Second Wright Company Factory

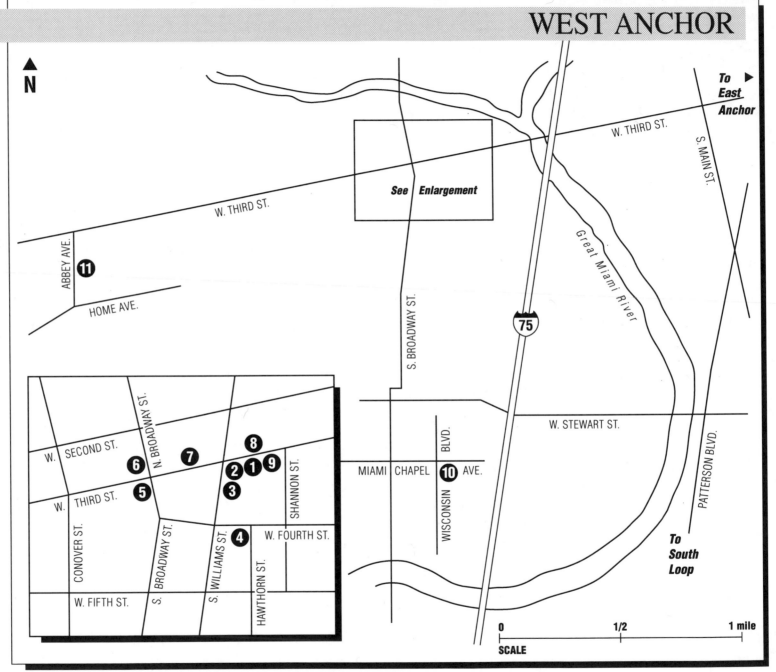

WEST ANCHOR

The Aviation Trail West Anchor (WA) includes the Dayton West Side neighborhood where Wilbur and Orville Wright lived and worked and invented the airplane, two locations of The Wright Company, formed by the brothers to manufacture their invention, and the Aviation Trail Museum and Visitors Center, the suggested starting point for a tour of the Trail.

The Wright brothers neighborhood sites are easily covered as a walking tour, allowing the visitor to "walk in the footsteps of Wilbur and Orville Wright." These include:

- The Wright family home site,
- Two locations of the brothers' job printing business, in which one of their associates was Paul Laurence Dunbar, a classmate of Orville who later became a famous black poet,
- Four locations of Wright bicycle shops, including the site of the shop in which they built the first airplane,
- And the site of Orville's laboratory.

The former Wright Company factory sites are now part of two General Motors Corporation Delphi Chassis Division plants. These are:

- The Wisconsin Boulevard plant, which is located partly on the site of the Speedwell Motor Car Company factory, where the Wrights rented space to build their first production airplanes,
- And the Home Avenue plant, which includes the two still-standing buildings erected by The Wright Company in 1910 and 1911.

The West Anchor serves as the western end of the *Pathway To Flight*, the route followed by the Wright brothers from their home on Dayton's West Side to their Huffman Prairie flying field east of Dayton, or the pathway from the beginning of flight in the Wrights' West Side Dayton bicycle shop to the aerospace projects of the future now being developed at Wright-Patterson Air Force Base, which includes the former Huffman Prairie flying field of Wilbur and Orville Wright.

Freefall parachute jump over McCook Field near the Great Miami River in the early 1920s. The freefall parachute was developed at McCook Field after World War I.

WA 1 Aviation Trail Museum and Visitors Center
1054 West Third Street
Dayton, Ohio 45407

A suggested starting point for a tour of the Aviation Trail is the Aviation Trail Museum and Visitors Center, which will be located on the first floor of a two-story modern structure being erected behind the preserved facade of a 1920s building known as the Stetzer building. Aviation Trail, Inc. offices and related facilities will be located on the second floor. The building is expected to be completed in 1997.

The visitors center will serve as an introduction and orientation point for the 47 sites that comprise the Aviation Trail; that is, the sites profiled in this book. The museum will include displays tracing the unique aviation history of the Dayton area, beginning with the invention of the airplane by Daytonians Wilbur and Orville Wright.

A major focus of the museum will be the Dave Gold parachute exhibit, based on the extensive collection of parachute expert Dave Gold, which was donated to Aviation Trail, Inc. by the Gold estate. This exhibit has particular relevance since Dayton is known as the "Birthplace of the Freefall Parachute" because it was developed at McCook Field (NL 1).

The first freefall parachute jump (a test jump) was made at McCook Field in 1919. McCook test pilot Harold R. Harris made the first emergency freefall parachute jump, in 1922 (see NL 2). And McCook test pilot John A. Macready made the first night emergency freefall parachute jump, in 1924 (see SL 2).

Aviation Trail, Inc. acquired the Setzer building in 1982 as part of the deal to purchase the adjacent historic Hoover Block building (WA 2). It emerged as a potential home for Aviation Trail, Inc. when the Dayton Aviation Heritage National Historical Park was created toward the end of 1992, since the legislation creating the park directed the National Park Service to acquire the Hoover Block, The Wright Cycle Company (WA 3) and the land in between -- property that Aviation Trail, Inc. owned and had been developing as a Wright brothers museum complex. This property was turned over to the National Park Service in January 1996, leaving Aviation Trail, Inc. without a permanent base.

The initial plan to restore the Setzer building for Aviation Trail, Inc.'s use was developed while the preliminary studies required before the park legislation was introduced were being completed. However, the restoration idea had to be scrapped after the rear portion of the building suddenly collapsed in the summer of 1992. A group of nearby workers were having their lunch break when they looked up and saw the building disintegrate before their eyes, leaving only the facade and a few feet behind it still standing. After the facade was stabilized and preserved, in 1994, plans were developed for a new two-story building behind it that would face on a plaza created to link it with the Hoover Block and The Wright Cycle Company. A groundbreaking for the new Aviation Trail building was held on November 3, 1995. The outer shell will be completed by the end of 1996 and the interior in 1997 as additional funds become available.

Aviation Trail, Inc. offices will remain at The Wright Cycle Company until the new building is completed.

WA 2 Hoover Block
1060 West Third Street
Dayton, Ohio 45407

Wilbur and Orville Wright once had a job printing business in the still-standing building known as the Hoover Block and the International Aeroplane Club of Dayton once met in Hoover Hall on the building's third floor.

The Wrights' job printing business, Wright and Wright, was located in a suite at the front of the second floor from the fall of 1890 to the spring of 1895. During this period, Wright and Wright printed *The Tattler*, a newspaper started by Paul Laurence Dunbar, later a famous black poet, published the Wrights' magazine *Snap Shots*, and filled various printing orders.

The Tattler, conceived by Dunbar as a weekly newspaper for blacks, was first issued December 13, 1890. According to Orville, a classmate of Dunbar at Central High School, publication of *The Tattler* continued "as long as our financial resources permitted of it, which was not long!" (Orville was then 19 years old and Dunbar 18.) Around the time of *The Tattler*'s publication, Dunbar is reported to have chalked on a wall of the printing shop the following poem:

> *Orville Wright is out of sight*
> *In the printing business.*
> *No other mind is half so bright*
> *As his'n is.*

The Wrights began publication of their weekly magazine *Snap Shots* on October 20, 1894, with publication continuing for about a year after they moved from the Hoover Block. The last issue, April 17, 1896, announced the beginning of the Wrights' bicycle manufacturing business with ". . .we will have several samples out in a week or ten days and will be ready to fill orders before the middle of next week."

Job printing appears to have been a major portion of the Wrights' business. Orders included the printing of minutes and reports of church conferences (many for the Church of the United Brethren in Christ), constitutions and by-laws of various church-related or civic organizations, advertisements and holiday menus. Among the more interesting jobs was the publication of an address by Bishop H. J. Becker, D. D., delivered at Hanby, Oregon on December 8, 1892, titled *Hindrances to the More Speedy Conversion of the World: An Address on Moral Reform*. Original examples of Wright and Wright printing can be found in the Wright Brothers Collection at Wright State University (EA 5).

In 1895 the Wrights moved their printing business to the still-standing building at 22 South Williams Street (WA 3), located directly behind the Hoover Block.

The International Aeroplane Club of Dayton held its monthly meetings in Hoover Hall starting in 1909. The club was organized by a group of West Side businessmen to honor their neighbors, Wilbur and Orville Wright, following the Wrights' triumphal 1908-1909 trip to Europe. Wilbur and Orville, their father and their brother Lorin often attended the club's meetings and social functions.

The Hoover Block in 1893. The sign "Wright and Wright Job Printing" appears on the second floor corner window. Part of the 22 South Williams building is visible at the extreme right of the picture. The Hoover Block picture was part of a collage of West Third Street buildings included in the book *New Dayton Illustrated*.

The Club was founded on May 13, 1909, the day Wilbur, Orville and Katharine Wright returned to Dayton following a trip to Europe, where Wilbur and Orville's flying demonstrations had made them international celebrities. Upon their return, the Wrights were greeted at the railroad station by thousands of Daytonians, then driven to their home on Hawthorn Street (WA 4) in a carriage drawn by four white horses. In the evening, a large crowd gathered around the Wright home for welcoming speeches and a fireworks display.

A month later, on June 16 and 17, the city of Dayton staged an elaborate two-day celebration in their honor. The festivities included a parade and drill by the Dayton Fire Department and a public reception at the Y.M.C.A. on the first day, and a ceremony at the Fairgrounds and a parade through downtown Dayton on the second day.

During the Fairgrounds ceremony, Wilbur and Orville were each presented with three gold medals: the Dayton Medal, presented by Mayor Edward E. Burkhart; the Ohio Medal, presented by Gover-

nor Judson Harmon; and the Congressional Medal, presented by General James Allen, Chief Signal Officer of the Army, representing President William H. Taft. The medals are now owned by Wright State University.

The parade that afternoon carried out the theme of "development of locomotion in America." Among the floats was one sponsored by The West Side Businessmen's Association that carried the legend, "The Wright brothers invention should prevent future wars and insure peace."

The three-story brick Hoover Block dates back to 1890 when it was erected by Zachary T. Hoover, the proprietor of a drug store across the street on the northeast corner of West Third and North Williams Streets. Frank B. Hale, who was married to Hoover's daughter Lura, a classmate of Orville Wright at Central High School, operated a grocery on the first floor from 1900 until World War I. Hale later served as mayor of Dayton from 1922 to 1926.

In 1982 the Hoover Block was purchased by Aviation Trail,

The West Side Business Men's float in the Wright homecoming parade, June 1909

West Dayton Reception Committee for the Wright homecoming in 1909, taken in the backyard of the Wright home. Left to right, standing: Prof. Cecil, John Neibert, Sam Rubenstein, Bishop Clippinger, Charles Grumbach, Walter Kuhns, Frank Hale, William Andrews, Frank Hamburger, William Kuhns, Lorin Wright, W. C. Reeder, Wilbur Wright, Webb Landis, Milton Wright, Albert Shearer, Lon Shank, Orville Wright, E. H. Sines, Charles Taylor, L. H. Hotchkiss, George McCullough and Bob Kelly; kneeling: Oscar Needham, William Kirschner, Joe Boyd, Billy Landis and Ed Ellis.

Inc., which made plans to restore it and open it as a museum that would include a major parachute exhibit. However, the legislation passed in 1992 creating the Dayton Aviation Heritage National Historical Park stipulated that the National Park Service was to acquire the Hoover Block, The Wright Cycle Company (WA 3) and the land in between. Consequently, ownership of the Hoover Block was transferred to the Park Service in January 1996.

The National Park Service plans to do an historical restoration of the Hoover Block when funds become available. In the meantime, murals representing how the building might have appeared in the 1890s have been installed on the outside of the structure. The murals, and similar ones across the street at the northwest corner, were provided through the efforts of The 2003 Committee, the local planning group for the Centennial of Flight celebration in 2003. The Committee also was the major force behind the establishment of the Dayton Aviation Heritage National Historical Park.

WA 3   The Wright Cycle Company
22 South Williams Street
Dayton, Ohio 45407

Wilbur and Orville Wright operated a bicycle shop and a job printing business in the still-standing building at 22 South Williams Street from 1895 to 1897. It was while occupying this building that the brothers took their first steps toward inventing the airplane.

Before gaining fame and fortune as the inventors of the airplane, Wilbur and Orville supported themselves with two businesses, a job printing business and a bicycle shop. The two enterprises were brought together under the same roof for the first time when both were moved to the 22 South Williams Street building in the spring of 1895.

The Wrights' printing business, Wright and Wright, was started by Orville in the family home (WA 4) while he was a student in high school. A few months later, in the spring of 1889, it was moved to a rented room at 1210 West Third Street (WA 5), then in the fall of 1890 to 1060 West Third Street (WA 2), where it remained until the move to South Williams.

While in the Williams Street building, Wright and Wright was managed mostly by Ed Sines, a longtime associate. The company filled printing orders and published the final year's issues of the Wrights' weekly magazine *Snap Shots*. The last issue of the magazine (April 17, 1896) carried an advertisement for the first bicycles manufactured under the Wright brothers' own brand names. As the Wrights' bicycle business increased, the importance of the printing business dwindled.

The Wrights' bicycle shop, opened in 1893 in a rented room at 1005 West Third Street (WA 8), at first was mainly the responsibility of Wilbur while Orville continued to spend most of his time at the printing shop. Less than a year after it opened, the bicycle shop was moved across the street to 1034 West Third Street (WA 9) where it remained until the move to 22 South Williams. Coincident with that move, the Wrights opened a second bicycle shop, at 23 West Second Street (CL 2), which closed about a year later.

Two significant events occurred during the years Wilbur and Orville occupied the 22 South Williams building: the death of Otto Lilienthal, a German aeronautics experimenter, and the expansion of their bicycle business from merely sales and repairs into the manufacture of their own brands.

Otto Lilienthal had been studying the problem of flight since 1879. Among his contributions were air pressure data (considered reliable at the time, but later found to be erroneous by the Wrights) and the development of 18 distinct glider types. Lilienthal's hang glider experiments in the 1890s, credited with popularizing aeronautics, were widely covered by the newspapers and magazines, which referred to him as the "winged Prussian." It was these articles about Lilienthal's activities that first aroused in Wilbur and Orville a serious interest in discovering the secrets of flight. Then, Lilienthal's death on August 10, 1896 from injuries received in a glider accident the day before, provided the emotional impetus that set them on the path to

The Wright Cycle Company at 22 South Williams Street in 1896. The bicycle shop is incidental to a photograph of another subject.

developing powered, controlled, manned flight, culminating in the invention of the airplane in 1903.

The Wright brothers began producing their own brands of bicycles in the spring of 1896. The first to appear was the Van Cleve model, named for their great-great-grandmother, Catharine Van Cleve Thompson, the first white woman to set foot in Dayton. Original Wright Van Cleve model bicycles are on display at Carillon Historical Park (SL 1) and the United States Air Force Museum (EA 1). The St. Clair, the second model manufactured by the Wrights, was named for Arthur St. Clair, one of the first four legal proprietors of Dayton along with James Wilkinson, Israel Ludlow and Jonathan Dayton. (The town was named after Dayton because the others thought his name sounded best.)

The experience gained while manufacturing their own brands

of bicycles proved invaluable to the Wright brothers in constructing their first airplane. Experimenting with a gas engine (fueled by piped illuminating gas often found in buildings of that era) to run the machinery in their bicycle shop provided skills they later applied in building the engine for their airplane. Experience with the chain drive on a bicycle aided them in designing the plane's power transmission from engine to propeller. Knowledge of parts suppliers and familiarity with local foundry capabilities enabled them to build the engine and complete the machine quickly when time was an important factor in order to test the airplane during the 1903 season. And, finally, the Wrights' bicycle shop was equipped with most of the needed machinery and tools.

During the years the Wright businesses were located on South Williams, Wilbur and Orville often were the sole occupants of the family home on Hawthorn Street while their father was travelling on church matters and their sister Katharine was away at Oberlin College in Oberlin, Ohio. During these periods, the brothers sometimes took their meals at a nearby boarding house in the still-standing building at 1126 West Third Street. At other times, they "self-boarded," taking turns doing their own cooking.

The two-story brick building at 22 South Williams dates back to 1886 when it was erected by brothers Abraham and Joseph Nicholas. The brothers operated a grocery store on the first floor for two years before selling the property to Joseph H. Hohler for $3,500 in 1888. Hohler had a grocery store, then a feed store on the first floor and lived with his family on the second floor until 1891. After that he rented the property, first as a saloon and boarding house, then to Wilbur and Orville Wright. The Wrights paid $16 per month for the entire building.

In 1982 Aviation Trail, Inc. purchased The Wright Cycle Company building with the intention of restoring it and opening it as a museum. By 1988 the exterior and first floor restoration had been completed, an exhibit about the Wright brothers installed on the first floor and the building opened as a museum.

After the Dayton Aviation Heritage National Historical Park

Wilbur Wright at work in the Wright bicycle shop at 22 South Williams Street in 1897.

was created in 1992, Aviation Trail, Inc. completed the second floor to serve as headquarters for the new park, which honors Wilbur and Orville Wright and their friend, poet Paul Laurence Dunbar. The park encompasses four scattered sites: the core site, consisting of The Wright Cycle Company, the Hoover Block and the land in between; the nearby Dunbar House Museum, 219 North P. L. Dunbar Street (see WA 9); the original Wright Flyer III and Wright Hall at Carillon Historical Park (SL 1); and the Wrights' Huffman Prairie Flying Field (EA 3) at Wright-Patterson Air Force Base.

In January 1996 ownership of The Wright Cycle Company was transferred to the National Park Service. The building is listed on the National Register of Historic Places and is a National Historic Landmark.

The first floor museum exhibits depict Wilbur and Orville

Wright's three businesses: printing, bicycles and airplanes. Among the displays is bicycle-manufacturing machinery similar to that used by the Wright brothers in their bicycle shop.

Hours are 8:00 a.m. to 5:00 p.m. Monday through Friday, 10:00 a.m. to 4:00 p.m. Saturday and noon to 4:00 p.m. Sunday from Memorial Day to Labor Day. The remainder of the year, hours are 10:00 a.m. to 4:00 p.m. Saturday and noon to 4:00 p.m. Sunday, or by appointment by telephoning 937-225-7706. Admission is free.

WA 4   Wright Family Home Site
7 Hawthorn Street
Dayton, Ohio 45407

The house in which Wilbur and Orville Wright lived when they invented the airplane once stood on the now vacant lot at 7 Hawthorn Street. The original house is an exhibit at Greenfield Village in Dearborn, Michigan.

The Wright family occupied the Hawthorn Street house during two periods: from 1871 to 1878 and from 1885 to 1914. In between, the family lived in Cedar Rapids, Iowa for three years (1878 to 1881), then in Richmond, Indiana for three years (1881 to 1884).

The Wright family first came to Dayton (from Hartsville, Indiana) in the spring of 1869 when Rev. Milton Wright was appointed editor of the weekly *Religious Telescope*, a Church of the United Brethren in Christ publication. At this time, the family consisted of Milton, his wife, Susan, and their sons, Reuchlin, age eight, Lorin, age six, and Wilbur, age two.

After living in rented houses for two years, the Wrights moved into the Hawthorn Street house in April 1871. Orville was born a few months later, on August 19, 1871, and Katharine exactly three years after Orville, on August 19, 1874. Twins Otis and Ida, born

The Wright family home at 7 Hawthorn Street in 1897.

February 2, 1870, lived only a few weeks and are buried in Greencastle Cemetery, at the corner of South Broadway Street and Miami Chapel Road. The Wright family's first stay in Dayton ended in June 1878 with Milton's transfer to Cedar Rapids, Iowa following his election as a bishop in 1877.

The Wright family returned to Dayton in June 1884 when Milton was appointed publisher of the *Christian Conservator*, another United Brethren publication. By this time Reuchlin was 23, Lorin, 21, Wilbur, 17, Orville, 12 and Katharine, nine. (Reuchlin and Lorin had been working in Dayton for about a year before the 1884 move,

Orville, left, and Wilbur Wright in France in 1909.

Reuchlin as a clerk and Lorin as a bookkeeper.) The family moved back to 7 Hawthorn Street in October 1885 after living in a rented house at 114 North Summit Street (now P. L. Dunbar Street) while waiting for the lease on their former home to expire.

Soon after reoccupying the Hawthorn Street house, the household began to dwindle. Reuchlin married in 1886 and moved to 1533 West Second Street, then settled in Kansas in 1890. Susan, who had been in ill health for several years, died of tuberculosis on July 4, 1889 at the age of 58. Lorin married in 1892 and moved to 117 South Horace Street, three blocks east of Hawthorn. And Wilbur died of typhoid fever on May 30, 1912 at the age of 45, two years before the new Wright home in Oakwood was completed. In April 1914 the three remaining members of the Hawthorn Street household: Orville, Katharine and Milton, moved to the new Wright mansion, Hawthorn Hill (SL 11), in the Dayton suburb of Oakwood.

Wilbur and Orville Wright invented the airplane during the family's second stay at the Hawthorn Street house. They accomplished this monumental feat in a little over seven years, beginning in 1896 when their interest in the problem of human flight was first aroused by reading about the glider experiments of Otto Lilienthal in Germany.

A combination of reading about what previous experimenters had discovered and observing the flight of birds at Pinnacle Hill (SL 7) led the Wrights to their initial breakthrough in 1899. This was the development of their wing-warping technique for lateral control. After discovering this final key to three-axis control, the brothers built a series of man-carrying experimental gliders, which they tested at Kitty Hawk, North Carolina in 1900, 1901 and 1902. Then, in 1903, they invented the airplane engine and the airplane propeller, which they added to a glider similar in design to their successful 1902 model to produce the world's first man-carrying powered airplane.

Not satisfied merely to prove man could fly, the Wrights continued to perfect the airplane by building two more experimental models, which they tested in 1904 and 1905 at Huffman Prairie (EA 3), their flying field east of Dayton.

After making the world's first sale of a military airplane, to the United States Army, the Wrights formed The Wright Company (see WA 10) at the end of 1909 to manufacture their invention. Proceeds from The Wright Company enabled the brothers to build Hawthorn Hill, planned by both Wilbur and Orville, but not completed until after Wilbur's death.

When the Wright family first came to Dayton, the neighborhood in which they settled was called Miami City and an Indian mound still stood on the north side of West Third Street four blocks east of Hawthorn. About a year later, the area's name was changed to the West Side after it was annexed to Dayton.

Milton Wright purchased the seven-room two-story frame house at 7 Hawthorn Street new for $1,800 in December 1870. Various alterations over the years included the addition of a front porch, built by Wilbur and Orville in 1892, and remodeling to change the arrangement of the rooms: a parlor, dining room and kitchen downstairs and four bedrooms upstairs.

The property included a shed at the rear where Wilbur and Orville set up a darkroom after they became interested in photography. Their photographic skills later enabled them to provide valuable photographic evidence of their accomplishments as they invented and perfected the airplane. Unfortunately, a number of their negatives, along with their early records, were damaged or destroyed in the disastrous 1913 Dayton flood that inundated much of the city, including the Hawthorn Street neighborhood. Many of the surviving photographs are now part of the Wright Brothers Collection at Wright State University (EA 5). Their camera, a Korona V manufactured by the Gundlach Optical Company of Rochester, New York, is on display at Carillon Historical Park (SL 1).

In 1900 Milton Wright deeded the Hawthorn Street property, then appraised at $2,500, to his daughter Katharine. (At the same time, he gave his 160-acre farm in Iowa to his four sons.) After the family moved to Hawthorn Hill in 1914, Katharine rented the house to Lottie (Charlotte) Jones, the Wrights' longtime laundress. Twenty years later Lottie Jones purchased the property for its appraised value of $3,500 when it was sold to settle Katharine's estate.

In November 1936 the Edison Institute acquired the property from Lottie Jones and moved the house, the shed in the rear and two feet of dirt from under the house to Greenfield Village in Dearborn, Michigan to serve as a memorial to Wilbur and Orville Wright. The restored family home was formally dedicated as an exhibit on April 16, 1938 in the presence of Orville Wright and other dignitaries.

WA 5   First Wright Brothers Printing Shop Site
1210 West Third Street
Dayton, Ohio 45407

The Wright brothers' first printing shop outside their home was located in a rented room at 1210 West Third Street, in a building that has since been demolished. The Wrights occupied the room from the spring of 1889 until the fall of 1890 when the business was moved to 1060 West Third Street (WA 2). While at 1210 West Third, the brothers published two newspapers, the *West Side News* and *The Evening Item*, and filled various printing orders.

The first issue of the weekly *West Side News* appeared March 1, 1889 while the business was still located in the family home at 7 Hawthorn Street (WA 4) but by the April 27, 1889 issue publication had been moved to the 1210 West Third Street address. The *West Side News* cost 50 cents for a one-year subscription or ten cents for ten weeks, later raised to ten cents for six weeks or 25 cents for three months. Content of the four-page paper was about half advertisements and about half local and general news items. Among the news items appearing in the March 30, 1889 issue was one illustrating the Wright sense of humor: "The city elections will be held Monday, April 1st. Vote early and often." The last issue of the *West Side News* appeared April 5, 1890.

The *West Side News* soon was followed by the daily *Evening Item*, first issued April 30, 1890. *The Evening Item*, published every day except Sunday, had the stated aim of being "a real newspaper devoted to the interests of the West Side." *The Evening Item* cost 25 cents for four weeks. Discontinued in August 1890, the paper lasted less than four months.

Original copies of the *West Side News* and *The Evening Item* are in the Dayton Collection at the Dayton-Montgomery County Public Library, 215 East Third Street, in downtown Dayton.

The Wrights' printing shop was the first of the brothers' three businesses: job printing, bicycles and airplanes. Although Wilbur and Orville may have been influenced by their father's occupation as an editor and publisher of the Church of the United Brethren in Christ publications, their original interest in the printing business appears to have grown from an attraction to the mechanics involved, including the operation and construction of the printing presses.

The initial interest in printing came from Orville, who first became interested in the process when he was 12 years old, shortly before the Wright family returned to Dayton in 1884. Curious about several woodprints he noticed in *Century Magazine*, Orville located some books describing the technique, then made his own woodblocks from materials he found around the house. Orville's approach to the woodcut problem illustrates the approach of the Wright brothers throughout their career: the combination of studying what others had done before and actual experience or experimentation.

When the Wright family returned to Dayton, Orville discovered that his friend Ed Sines, who lived at 15 Hawthorn Street, also was interested in printing and owned a small press. The two formed a partnership, Sines and Wright, and advertised that they would "do job printing cheaper than any other firm in town."

In 1886 Sines and Wright started publication of *The Midget*, a weekly "journal devoted to the interests of the Intermediate School," printed in the Wright home. Apparently the first issue of April 1886 also was the last. Among the news stories in *The Midget* was one concerning a group of workers striking against the Malleable Iron Works, who overturned a railroad car on the Third Street Railroad when the company attempted to run a train "in opposition of the strikers."

The Sines and Wright partnership broke up over a disagreement on what to do with the profits from one of their printing jobs. In this case the customer had paid in popcorn. Orville wanted to sell the popcorn and use the proceeds to buy more type but Ed wanted to pop the popcorn and eat it. The disagreement was resolved by Orville buying out Ed. Sines continued to be associated with the Wright printing business until it was sold in 1899, but as an employee, not as an owner. In an interview in 1938, Ed Sines said of the Wright brothers, "had they not invented the airplane the boys would have invented something else."

Orville continued to be interested in the mechanics of the printing process, building several presses and teaching himself how to make stereotype plates so he could reuse his limited supply of type to fill larger printing orders. And to increase his knowledge of the business, he spent two summer vacations working 60 hours a week at a local printing company.

Shortly after Orville started the *West Side News* toward the end of his junior year in high school, Wilbur joined him in the business, which then became Wright and Wright. By his senior year Orville had become so absorbed in the printing business that he attended classes only a few hours a day, thus never earning enough credits to graduate.

Although Wilbur had qualified for a high school diploma before the family moved back to Dayton in June 1884, he chose not to return to Richmond, Indiana for the graduation ceremony. Between June 1884 and the spring of 1889, when he joined Orville in Wright and Wright, Wilbur attended post-graduate courses at Central High School and helped care for his ailing mother, who died in 1889. He also battled health problems for several years, including a heart disorder and facial injuries received when he was hit with a hockey stick during an ice hockey game at the Old Soldiers' Home on West Third Street. The Old Soldiers Home is now called the Veterans Administration (VA) Medical Center. The lake is part of a park near the main entrance at Gettysburg and Lakeview Avenues.

The building that housed the Wright brothers first printing shop outside their home was torn down in the 1950s. The property is now owned by Bank One, which has developed it as a parking lot for its West Third Street branch, across the street on the southeast corner of South Broadway and West Third Streets.

WA 6   Orville Wright's Laboratory Site
15 North Broadway Street
Dayton, Ohio 45407

Orville Wright's laboratory, which he occupied from 1916 until his death in 1948, once stood on the now vacant lot at 15 North Broadway Street. Called the Wright Aeronautical Laboratory, the Broadway Street building was constructed for Orville's personal use. Here he conducted fundamental scientific research, carried out consulting projects during World War I and developed the split-wing flap.

Among Orville's World War I projects was work on the propeller for the first guided missile, called the *Bug*, which was developed at the Dayton Wright Airplane Company Experimental Station (SL 3), where Orville was a consulting engineer. Orville also served in the Signal Officers Reserve Corps after being commissioned a major in the Aviation Section in 1917.

The split-wing flap, developed while Orville was a consulting engineer for Dayton Wright, initially was pronounced to be of "no value" in a January 1922 Navy Bureau of Aeronautics report. Ten years later, the Navy became one of the first to use it. The split-wing flap helped prevent stalls, then a major cause of fatal airplane accidents, and also made dive-bombing possible. The split-wing flap was one of the two major contributions to aviation made by Orville after the death of his brother Wilbur in 1912. The other was his automatic stabilizer, which he demonstrated at Huffman Prairie (EA 3) on December 31, 1913, making seven consecutive turns without touching the controls of the airplane, a demonstration that earned him the Collier Trophy for 1913.

It has been noted that many of the early improvements to the airplane came from other than the original inventors, Wilbur and Orville Wright; for example, the first use of wheels rather than skids, the use of tractor propulsion rather than pusher, the first hydroplane and the closed cockpit. Part of the explanation may lie in the early death of Wilbur in 1912, which broke up the intellectual interaction between the two brothers that had stimulated their thinking and led to

Orville Wright's office at his laboratory at 15 North Broadway Street.

original solutions to fundamental problems. But part of the explanation also may lie in the time-and-energy-consuming efforts of the Wrights to protect their financial interests by pursuing a series of patent suits, as well as efforts to insure they received due recognition as the inventors of the airplane, including a long-lasting controversy between Orville and the Smithsonian Institution.

The Smithsonian Institution controversy centered around the Smithsonian's refusal to acknowledge Wilbur and Orville Wright as the inventors of the airplane, contending instead that the honor should go to Dr. Samuel P. Langley, a director and secretary of the Institution. In retaliation, Orville refused to allow the Wright Flyer I to be put on permanent display in the United States.

The Smithsonian's position was based on a test of the Langley machine made on December 8, 1903, nine days before the Wrights' December 17th Kitty Hawk flights. Langley's aeronautical experiments, which were supported by several grants, including $50,000 from the United States government and $20,000 from the Hodgkins fund, dated back to his model powered airplanes flown in 1896. The December 8th test was intended to prove Langley's theories on a man-carrying machine designed by Langley. The pilot, Charles M. Man-

Orville Wright's laboratory at 15 North Broadway Steet around 1930.

ley, had developed the plane's engine and also was Langley's assistant.

On the day of the December 8th test, Manley optimistically attached a compass to his pants leg so he could find his way back if he became lost on the flight. As it turned out, Manley had no need for the compass because the guy wires of the Langley-designed airplane broke the moment it rose from its launching site on a houseboat on the Potomac River near Washington, D.C., plunging the machine and its pilot into the river. In spite of what most would consider to be an unsuccessful test, the Smithsonian installed the Langley machine as an exhibit, with its designer identified as the inventor of the airplane.

Over the years various attempts were made to resolve the Wright-Smithsonian disagreement, including an attempt initiated by Alexander Graham Bell after the first public display of the Wright Flyer I at the Massachusetts Institute of Technology in June 1916. When approached by Bell, then-secretary of the Smithsonian Dr. Charles Walcott showed great reluctance to display the Wright plane, which had flown, alongside the Langley plane, which had not.

Finally convinced that the Smithsonian was uninterested in negotiating a solution to the recognition problem, Orville Wright agreed to a request to exhibit the Flyer I at the Science Museum,

South Kensington, London, England. Subsequently, in 1928 the Flyer I was shipped to England where it remained until shortly after Orville's death in 1948.

The final resolution to the controversy came in 1942 with the Smithsonian's publication of a brochure titled *The 1914 tests of the Langley "Aerodrome,"* which contained apologies and retractions satisfactory to Orville. With Orville's consent, arrangements eventually were made after the end of World War II to bring the Wright airplane back to the United States. On December 17, 1948 the Flyer I was dedicated as an exhibit at the Smithsonian Institution, 45 years after Orville Wright made the world's first manned powered flight.

Orville Wright's laboratory was a one-story brick and concrete block building erected in 1916 on a lot that had been purchased by both brothers in 1909. The front of the building contained an office presided over by Mabel Beck, Orville's secretary. To the rear was the laboratory, set up like a machine shop with a workbench running along the walls. Equipment included the three-foot wind tunnel built by Orville that is now on display at the United States Air Force Museum (EA 1).

Orville Wright sold the 15 North Broadway Street property in 1919 and thereafter rented the building from its succeeding owners until his death. Orville died at the age of 76 on January 30, 1948, three days after suffering a heart attack at his laboratory.

Orville's laboratory was part of a tract purchased by Sohio in 1971 with the intention of clearing the land and erecting a gas station. Realizing the historic nature of the laboratory, Sohio offered the building to any civic group who would move the structure and arrange for its maintenance. Although several groups pursued the matter, none was able to raise the necessary funds. Finally, in 1976, the laboratory was demolished to clear the land. However, soon after the demolition, Sohio abandoned its plans and the gas station was never built. The property, developed as green space, is now owned by Bank One.

WA 7   Last Wright Brothers Bicycle Shop Site
1127 West Third Street
Dayton, OH 45407

The bicycle shop in which Wilbur and Orville Wright built the world's first airplane once stood at 1127 West Third Street. The original building is now an exhibit at Greenfield Village in Dearborn, Michigan. A replica of the building, dedicated in 1972, is at Carillon Historical Park (SL 1).

The Wright brothers moved their printing and bicycle businesses from 22 South Williams Street (WA 3) to the west half of a remodeled dwelling at 1127 West Third Street in the fall of 1897. There the brothers gradually phased out their original enterprises as the importance of their aviation business grew.

The Wrights sold their printing business in 1899 when their longtime employee Ed Sines was forced to leave after being injured in an accident. One of the last publications was *Van Cleve Notes*, a promotional newsletter put out by The Wright Cycle Company. The May 8, 1899 issue advertised two second hand Van Cleve bicycles, one for $20 and one for $18, and contained a notice that the 1898 model St. Clair bicycles were being closed out at $25.

The Wright Cycle Company stopped manufacturing bicycles in 1904 (the year after the Wrights became the first to fly) and went out of business altogether in 1908. Another Dayton Company, W. F. Meyers, later manufactured bicycles under the Van Cleve brand name into the 1930s.

From 1909 on the Wrights devoted all of their time to their "aeroplane" enterprises, at first doing business under the name Wright Brothers at the 1127 West Third Street address. Even after organizing The Wright Company and building a new factory (WA 11) farther out on West Third Street, the brothers continued to maintain offices in the 1127 West Third Street building, Wilbur until his death in 1912 and Orville until he moved around the corner to his new laboratory at 15 North Broadway Street (WA 6) in 1916.

Wilbur and Orville Wright built the world's first airplane in a machine shop set up in a wooden shed attached to the rear of the building at 1127 West Third. In inventing the airplane, the brothers had to solve four major problems: how to maintain control on three axes, how to provide lift sufficient for sustained flight, how to provide power, and how to provide propulsion. The Wrights' solution to the problem of three-axis control is described under the Pinnacle Hill site (SL 7), where the brothers' observations of the flight of birds led to the development of their wing-warping theory for lateral control, a principle still used in the present-day aileron system.

The Wrights worked out the problem of lift by experimenting with a series of man-carrying gliders in 1900, 1901 and 1902. In designing their first glider the brothers relied upon the work of preceding experimenters. Englishman Sir George Cayley (born in 1773), known as "the father of aerial navigation," was the first to suggest using an arched rather than a flat wing. F. H. Wenham, co-inventor of the wind tunnel in 1871, had proposed using multiple planes rather than a single plane, based on his wind tunnel tests. (The Wrights' gliders and airplane were all biplanes.) Horatio F. Phillips had developed the cambered airfoil (a two-surface wing with the curve on top greater than the curve on the bottom). And Otto Lilienthal had formulated theoretical air pressure tables in 1889, which the Wrights used to calculate their wing areas. The breakthrough in solving the problem of lift came when the Wrights found Lilienthal's air pressure tables to be inaccurate following the disappointing performance of their second glider during tests at Kitty Hawk, North Carolina in 1901.

Back at their Dayton machine shop, the brothers conducted scientific experiments to formulate their own air pressure tables, data which they then used in designing their successful 1902 glider and all of their subsequent machines. A Wright Van Cleve model bicycle equipped with a horizontal wheel to which model airfoils are attached, as in the brothers' first air pressure table experiments, and a model of the wind tunnel they constructed for later tests are on display at Carillon Historical Park (SL 1).

After the successful tests of their third glider at Kitty Hawk in 1902, the brothers faced two unexpected problems: no established manufacturer was able, or willing, to produce an engine to power their glider, and marine propellers proved to be unsuitable for an airplane.

How the brothers invented the airplane engine is described under the Engineer's Club site (CL 4), where the Wright engine number three is on display.

The first Wright engine, which powered the 1903 Flyer I, was built to the brothers' design by the Wrights' chief bicycle mechanic, Charley Taylor, who used a lathe and drill press as his only powered tools. Taylor later became a Wright Company airplane mechanic. Charles E. Taylor (1868-1956) was inducted into the National Aviation Hall of Fame (see EA 1) in 1965.

The Wright brothers invented the airplane propeller after they found a marine propeller could not be adapted to their needs because, as Orville later wrote in a letter to the Dayton Public Library dated March 3, 1947, ". . . the marine engineers of that time did not base their calculations of screw propellers on a theory but entirely on empirical formulae."

The Wrights' breakthrough in solving the propulsion problem was their realization that the propeller was essentially an airfoil, a rotating wing that grasped the air to move the machine forward, thus converting the energy produced by the engine into a propulsive force. The brothers' first propellers, the two installed on their 1903 Flyer 1, were rather crudely fashioned by hacking them out of a block of lami-

The Wright bicycle shop at 1127 West Third Street around 1909. The Wright brothers built the world's first airplane here in 1903.

nated spruce wood with an ax, then shaping them to specifications with a drawknife. Power was transmitted from the engine by a chain running over a sprocket as in a bicycle.

The world's first airplane, the Wright Flyer I, incorporated the Wright brothers' solutions to the problems of control, lift, power and propulsion, principles that are still employed by the airplanes of today. On the day they made the first manned powered flights,

December 17, 1903, Wilbur was 36 years old and Orville 32. The Flyer I is now on display at the Smithsonian Institution in Washington, D. C.

Wilbur Wright (1867-1912) and Orville Wright (1871-1948) were inducted into the National Aviation Hall of Fame in 1962.

Wilbur and Orville Wright invented the airplane without any outside financial assistance. The brothers' total cash outlay, including their railroad fares to and from Kitty Hawk, was reported to be less than $1,000, all provided out of the profits of their bicycle business. Their only other source of income during this period was their share of the proceeds from the 1901 sale of a farm in Iowa given to them and their two older brothers by their father in 1900. As an Engineers Club president once said of the first airplane, "Its builders had no multi-billion dollar appropriation or budget, no vast laboratory or factory in which to build it. They did it in their shop, with their hands and their minds, using ancient tools and crude materials."

The building that housed the Wright brothers' last bicycle shop was a former two-story brick residence that had been converted into two storefronts just prior to the Wrights' occupancy. The other store, on the east side, was occupied by an undertaker. The building was owned by Charles Webbert, who had a plumbing business at 1121 West Third Street.

In 1936 the Edison Institute purchased the building at 1127 West Third as a display for Greenfield Village, an open air American history museum at Dearborn, Michigan founded by Henry Ford in 1929. Before shipping the building to its new site, the historic structure was carefully dismantled and each piece systematically marked according to a diagram: for example, each floor board was identified by the letter "F" followed by a number in the sequence in which it was removed.

The restored Wright bicycle shop, together with the Wright family home (WA 4), was dedicated as an exhibit at Greenfield Village on April 16, 1938 in the presence of Orville Wright and other notables. Daytonian Charles F. Kettering, then president of the General Motors Research Corporation, was the toastmaster at a dinner at the Dearborn Inn following the dedication ceremony.

A one-story building originally constructed as a drug store in 1951 now occupies the site of the Wright brothers last bicycle shop.

WA 8   First Wright Brothers Bicycle Shop Site
1005 West Third Street
Dayton, Ohio 45407

The Wright brothers' first bicycle shop was located at 1005 West Third Street, in a building that has since been incorporated into the Gem City Ice Cream Company building.

The Wrights entered the bicycle business in 1892, a few months after each purchased one of the new Safety bicycles: Orville, a new Columbia for $160 and Wilbur, a second hand Eagle bought at auction for $80. Realizing the potential of the new vehicle, the brothers rented space at 1005 West Third Street in December 1892 in preparation for opening a shop in the spring to sell bicycles and "cycle sundries." Called the Wright Cycle Exchange, the shop was an immediate success, forcing the brothers to move to larger quarters across the street at 1034 West Third Street (WA 9) a few months after they started the business.

The Wright brothers were fortunate in their choice of a business enterprise. The timing was right -- they entered the business at the beginning of the great 1890s bicycle boom and made their first flight on December 17, 1903, just as the boom was ending -- and the seasonal nature of the business allowed ample time for their aeronautical experiments in the off season. The profits from the business provided the funds to support their search for powered flight, including building their first airplanes.

The bicycle dates back to 1791 when the French Count de Sivrac invented what was later called the Hobby Horse, a wooden frame mounted on two wheels that the rider pushed with his feet. Pedals, mounted on the hub of the front wheel, were added in 1861 when another Frenchman, Ernest Michaux, introduced the Boneshaker.

Improvements followed rapidly once pedals were invented. The Ordinary, or High Wheeler, with a large front wheel and a small rear wheel, appeared in 1871; the Solid Tire Safety, with equal size wheels and a rear-wheel chain drive, in 1885; and, finally, in 1892, the prototype of the modern bicycle, the Cushion Tire Safety, equipped with the new pneumatic tires invented by Irishman John Dunlop in 1889. The 1892 Safety offered many advantages over the earlier attempts at designing personal transportation: speed, a safe and comfortable ride, easy operation and easy mounting and dismounting, making it suitable for women and children as well as men.

The Safety bicycle brought about a radical change in the lifestyle of Americans by providing ordinary men and women access to personal transportation equipment for the first time. In fact, the bicycle has been called the "first step in the emancipation of women," bringing with it less restrictive women's clothing and a new freedom to venture out of the home. So great was the appeal during the "Golden Age of the Bicycle" (1890-1900) that families cut back on necessities, even food, in order to purchase one of the new vehicles.

As the bicycle craze grew, cyclists began to organize clubs to defend their rights (for example, women cyclists often were dragged into court and charged with improper dress); to promote the need for more and better roads (ruts cause accidents); and to sponsor cycling events. Wilbur and Orville were members of one of the oldest of these, the League of American Wheelmen, which is still in existence today.

As a member of the Dayton chapter of the Wheelmen, Orville participated in many of the races sponsored by the club, winning at least three medals: for a half-mile race, a one-mile race and a two-mile race. The medals are on display at Carillon Historical Park (SL 1). Members of the Wheelmen, headquartered in the basement of the Y.M.C.A. (then located at 32-34 East Fourth Street), agreed to "make no club runs or use the club uniform on Sunday."

The building at 1005 West Third Street in which the Wright brothers had their first bicycle shop later housed the Gem City Ice Cream Company, started in 1901. The first commercial manufacturer of ice cream in Dayton, Gem City was a leading local ice cream maker for 70 years, until the operation was moved out of town after being purchased by an Akron, Ohio company in 1971.

The site is now occupied by a two-story brick building constructed by the Gem City Ice Cream Company in 1927. It incorporates the building that housed the Wright brothers' bicycle shop into the east end, with some the structural features of the original building still discernible inside the present building.

WA 9   Second Wright Brothers Bicycle Shop Site
1034 West Third Street
Dayton, Ohio 45407

Wilbur and Orville Wright's second bicycle shop was located in a rented store at 1034 West Third Street, in a building that has since been demolished. First opened across the street at 1005 West Third Street (WA 8), the shop was moved to 1034 West Third in May 1893 when increased business brought a need for larger quarters. Sometime after the move the name was changed from Wright Cycle Exchange to Wright Cycle Company.

While in the 1034 West Third Street shop, the Wrights sold various brands of bicycles and operated a repair service. Brands for sale included Coventry Cross, Halladay-Temple, Warwick, Reading, Smalley, Envoy, Duchess and Fleetwing. Prices ranged from about $40 for a boy's model up to $100 for a top quality adult bicycle. Fees from three rental bicycles brought in about $25 per month.

Wilbur exhibited a flair for advertising about this time when he came up with a scheme to attract the interest of high school students by distributing what appeared to be a purloined set of examination questions. Upon close inspection, however, the student quickly found that all of the questions concerned the bicycles on sale at the Wrights' bicycle shop.

During this period the Wrights gave one of the bicycles from

Central High School class of 1890. Paul Laurence Dunbar and Orville Wright are in the back row, Dunbar at the far left and Orville to the right of the two girls.

their shop to their friend Paul Laurence Dunbar. Dunbar used the bicycle, a Viking manufactured by the Union Manufacturing Company of Toledo, Ohio, as transportation from his home at 140 West Ziegler Street to his job as an elevator "conductor" in the Callahan Building, on the northeast corner of Third and Main Streets, now replaced by the National City Bank office building. Orville Wright and Dunbar were classmates at Central High School, on the southwest corner of Fourth and Wilkinson Streets, where the Senior Citizens Center now stands.

Paul Laurence Dunbar, an internationally famous black poet, was born in Dayton on June 27, 1872 to Matilda and Joshua Dunbar, former slaves from Kentucky. Joshua was Matilda's second husband and 20 years older than she.

The only black in his class at Central High School, Dunbar received strong support from his teachers and fellow students in the pursuit of his literary interests. While at Central, Dunbar was a member of the school's literary society and served as president in his senior year. He also was on the staff of the school paper, serving as editor in his senior year, and wrote the lyrics for the class song. Dunbar's literary interests complemented Orville Wright's interest in printing, leading to friendship between the two and to Dunbar's association with the Wrights in their printing business (see WA 2).

After graduation from high school, Dunbar became an elevator operator at the Callahan Building, the only job open to him at that time. Gradually, however, his writing found an audience, bringing in enough income for him to quit the elevator position and be listed as a "journalist" starting with the 1894-95 *Dayton Directory*.

Dunbar's first book of poems, *Oak and Ivy*, published in 1892 when he was 20 years old, and his second, *Majors and Minors* (1896), were both privately printed. His first commercially-published book was *Lyrics of Lowly Life* (containing 105 poems), published by Dodd, Mead and Company in 1896. From then on, Dunbar's reputation grew rapidly as he published additional volumes of poetry, novels and short stories and wrote the lyrics for several Broadway musicals. His reputation was further enhanced by his poetry readings before audiences across the United States and in Europe.

A major disappointment in Dunbar's life was the failure in 1902 of his four-year marriage to Alice Ruth Moore, a college-educated black woman, a failure stemming partly from Dunbar's health problems after he contracted tuberculosis in 1899.

Dunbar died at his home in Dayton on February 9, 1906 at the age of 33 -- the first of his race to achieve international acclaim as a literary figure. Not until two years later did his friends Wilbur and Orville Wright begin to receive notice for their own achievements following their flying demonstrations in Europe in 1908-1909. Dunbar is buried in Woodland Cemetery (SL 12), a short distance away from the Wright family plot.

The bicycle given to Dunbar by the Wright brothers is on display at the Dunbar House State Memorial complex, 219 P. L. Dunbar Street (formerly Summit Street), off West Third Street a few blocks west of the Wrights' businesses. The Dunbar House itself is one of the four Dayton Aviation Heritage National Historical Park sites (see WA 3). Dunbar bought the house for his mother Matilda after he attained success and lived there with her the last two years of his life. The house still contains much of the original furnishings displayed in their original settings.

The Dunbar House State Memorial complex is owned and operated by the Ohio Historical Society. The House is a National Historic Landmark.

The building at 1034 West Third Street that housed the Wrights' second bicycle shop was remodeled in the early 1900s into a two-story brick commercial building, which was demolished around 1980 after much of the structure was destroyed by fire.

The site is now a vacant lot owned by the City of Dayton. The city has developed it as green space to enhance the building next door to the east, restored by the city to serve as its Innerwest Priority Board office.

WA 10 First Wright Company Factory Site
Delphi Chassis Division Wisconsin Operations
General Motors Corporation
1420 Wisconsin Boulevard
Dayton, Ohio 45408

In 1909 Wilbur and Orville Wright organized The Wright Company to manufacture their invention. The first models, the Model B and the Model R, were produced in rented space at the Speedwell Motor Car Company factory, in a building that has since been demolished. The site is now occupied by the General Motors Delphi Chassis Division Wisconsin Operations High Bay Building.

The Speedwell plant was used from February 1910 until the Wright Company's new factory (WA 11) was completed in November 1910. During this period the engines were built in the Wrights' bicycle shop on West Third Street (WA 7) and trucked to the Speedwell facility for installation in the planes.

The Model B, the first mass produced airplane and the first Wright airplane without a front elevator, was a two-seat dual control biplane with a wheel-and-skid undercarriage. Built from 1910 to 1911, the plane was eight feet high and 29 feet long and had a 39-foot wing span and two eight-and-one-half-foot pusher propellers. It weighed 800 pounds and sold for $5,000. The first Model B was completed June 29, 1910.

A Model B was among the three airplanes purchased by the United States Navy in 1911 with its first airplane appropriation of $25,000. Two Model Bs were among the five machines purchased the same year by the United States Army with its second airplane appropriation, also $25,000. (The Army had purchased a Wright Model A for $30,000 in 1909 with its first appropriation.) The Model B also was used by the Wright exhibition flying team (see CL 6), to train students at the Wrights' Huffman Prairie flying school (EA 3) and to make the world's first commercial flight.

The first commercial flight, on November 7, 1910, was especially significant because it demonstrated the freight-carrying potential of the new invention. The flight was made by Wright Company pilot Philip O. Parmalee, who carried ten bolts of silk tied to his machine from Huffman Prairie to the Morehouse-Martens Department Store in Columbus, Ohio. An automobile transferred the cargo from the landing site to the store in downtown Columbus, foreshadowing present-day air freight deliveries. Parmalee made the 62-mile flight in 66 minutes, besting the time made by a competing Big Four Railroad express train. Morehouse-Martens paid a shipping charge of $5,000, but made a $1,000 profit by selling pieces of the fabric as souvenirs.

A modified 1911 Model B is on display at the United States Air Force Museum (EA 1) and a group of local aviation enthusiasts has constructed a flyable look-alike (see SL 8).

The Model R, also called the Baby Wright, the Baby Grand and the Roadster, was a one-place racing machine designed for speed and altitude competition. Model R flying records included four world altitude marks made by Wright exhibition flying team members in 1910. These ranged from a height of 4,384 feet, set on June 13 at Indianapolis, Indiana by Walter Brookins, to 9,714 feet, set on October 31 at Belmont Park, New York by Ralph Johnstone.

Daytonians had their first organized opportunity to view the new Wright Company airplanes September 19-24, 1910 during the city's Industrial Exposition and Fall Festival. The program included daily exhibitions at the Wright Huffman Prairie flying field and special flights on Aviation Day.

The Wright Company was incorporated November 22, 1909 by Wilbur and Orville Wright and a group of New York bankers, including Andrew Freedman, Alpheus F. Barnes, Russell A. Alger, August Belmont and Cornelius Vanderbilt. Wilbur was president and Orville, one of two vice presidents. The Wrights received $100,000 cash, 40 per cent of the stock and a ten per cent royalty on every airplane sold for assigning their American patent rights to the company. The Wright Company maintained a New York office at 527 Fifth Avenue but all manufacturing was done at the Dayton factory.

The Wright Company proved to be a profitable enterprise,

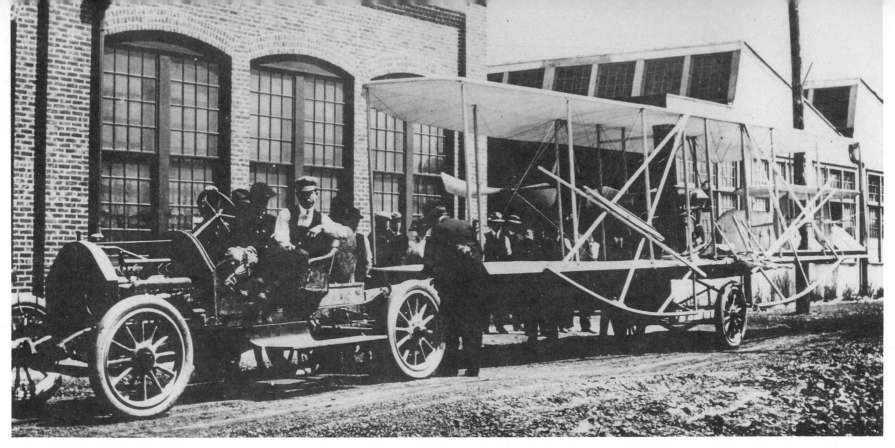

The Speedwell Motor Car Company factory where The Wright Company rented space in 1910 to manufacture its first model, the Model B. A disassembled Model B is shown leaving the factory.

earning more than $1,000,000 in 1911-1912 from exhibition flying team fees plus a few airplane sales. Wilbur and Orville Wright's financial situation improved dramatically. Between September 1909 and the end of 1910, from their American dealings alone, the brothers received $30,000 for the first United States Army airplane, $100,000 for forming The Wright Company, more than $50,000 in dividends and royalties, and $15,000 for Wilbur's flight in connection with the Hudson-Fulton Celebration in New York.

The 1909 Hudson-Fulton Celebration was a two-week celebration of two anniversaries: the 300th anniversary of the discovery of the Hudson River by Henry Hudson in 1609 and the 100th anniversary of the first trip up the river by Robert Fulton's steamship *Clermont* in 1807. Although the *Clermont* anniversary was off by two years, the Commission decided to combine the two events in one celebration. Among Wilbur's most spectacular flights during the festivities was his flight on October 4, in which he flew from Governor's Island, New York 20 miles up the Hudson River to Grant's Tomb and back in about one-half hour. An unusual aspect of the flight was the red canoe fastened between the skids of his airplane, its open top covered with canvas to make it watertight so it could act as a pontoon should the plane be forced to land on the water.

Wilbur and Orville also organized several European companies, but none was as successful as their American venture, possibly because they were unable to personally oversee the foreign operations.

Among their European enterprises were a French company, formed in 1908; the German Flugmaschine Wright Gesellschaft, formed in 1909; and the British Wright Company, Limited, formed by Orville in 1913. By the time Orville sold his 2,500 founder's shares in the French company in 1920, they brought only $1,800.

The Speedwell Motor Car Company factory was a one-story brick building with a sawtooth roofline typical of the factories of that time. The building, which previously had housed the Dayton Machine Tool Company, stood on the east side of Essex Avenue, now renamed Wisconsin Boulevard.

The Speedwell Motor Car Company was established in 1907 by Pierce D. Schenck. By 1911 the growing company was making a machine advertised as "a beautiful car which realizes every expectation aroused by its distinguished appearance." A seven-passenger touring model sold for $2,000. Two years later much of Speedwell's stock and equipment was damaged in the 1913 Dayton flood. The company failed to recover from the loss and went out of business in 1915. A restored 1910 Speedwell touring car is on display at Carillon Historical Park (SL 1).

According to Gilbert J. Loomis, Speedwell automotive designer, the Wrights frequently were offered automobile rides out to their Huffman Prairie flying field; however, the brothers always refused, believing automobiles to be "too dangerous," and chose instead to make the trip by traction car.

The Delphi Chassis Wisconsin Operations plant dates back to 1923 when Moraine Products was established at the General Motors Research Laboratories, located in part of what is now the General Motors Moraine Engine Plant (SL 5). The new company's first product was self-oiling powder metal bearings, an off-shoot of a research project at the laboratories. In 1937 Moraine Products moved to a new building on Wisconsin Boulevard next to Delco Brake, which had moved there the previous year after being spun off from Delco Products. Moraine Products and Delco Brake merged in 1942 under the name Delco Products, changed to Delco Moraine in 1960. In 1991 Delco Moraine, which had merged with Delco Products earlier, became part of the new Delphi Chassis Division. Today, the Wiscon-

Wilbur Wright adjusting the engine of his airplane at the Hudson-Fulton Celebration in New York in 1909. The canoe attached to the machine was intended to keep the airplane afloat in case he should be forced down while flying over water.

sin Operations plant manufactures brake systems for the automotive industry.

The building in which the first Wright Company airplanes were manufactured was replaced by the Delco Moraine High Bay Building in 1964. A plaque commemorating the site's historical significance was presented to Delco Moraine by Aviation Trail, Inc. at a community dinner on September 15, 1983, in celebration of General Motors' 75th anniversary. The plaque is installed by an entrance to the plant's offices on Wisconsin Boulevard, to the north of the High Bay Building.

The Delphi Chassis Wisconsin Operations plant is not open to the public.

WA 11   Former Second Wright Company Factory
Delphi Chassis Division Home Avenue Operations
General Motors Corporation
2701 Home Avenue
Dayton, Ohio 45417

The Wright Company and Plant 3 of the Dayton Wright Airplane Company once occupied the two buildings now known as Building 1 and Building 2 of the Delphi Chassis Division Home Avenue Operations.

Plant 3 of the Dayton Wright Airplane Company was located in the two buildings from 1917 until 1923 when they were taken over by the newly-organized Inland Manufacturing Company. Dayton Wright, formed by Edward A. Deeds and Charles F. Kettering to manufacture warplanes for World War I, is described under SL 5, the site of the company's main plant in the Dayton suburb of Moraine. Plant 3 manufactured small parts for Dayton Wright airplanes, including steering wheels and metal fittings.

Buildings 1 and 2 originally were constructed by The Wright Company to manufacture Wright airplanes. Organized by Wilbur and Orville Wright and a group of New York financiers at the end of 1909, The Wright Company initially rented manufacturing space at the Speedwell Motor Car Company plant (WA 10) until its new factory building (Building 1) was completed in November 1910. Upon the completion of a second building (Building 2) a year later the Wright factory had the capacity to produce four airplanes per month, a capacity greater than that of any other airplane factory in the world at that time.

The Wright Company production model airplanes were named after the letters of the alphabet starting with the Model A, the model sold to the United States Signal Corps in 1909. The Model B, the world's first mass-produced airplane, and the Model R, a racer, were first manufactured in the rented space at the Speedwell plant and are described under that site.

The first models manufactured exclusively at the company's own factory, the present-day Delphi Chassis Home Avenue plant buildings, were the Model EX, Model C and Model D. Later Wright Company models included the Models CH, E, F, G, H, HS, K and L.

The Model EX (1911) was a single-seat version of the Model B that was popular with exhibition pilots.

Models C and D (1912), equipped with 50-horsepower Wright engines, were produced in both civilian and military versions. The United States Army purchased seven of the two-seat Model Cs and two of the single-seat Model Ds for use as scouting airplanes. According to The Wright Company catalog, the Model C sold for $5,000 and "all 1912 models contained improvements suggested by Orville Wright" after his 1911 fall experiments at Kitty Hawk, North Carolina. Orville had experimented with a new glider at Kitty Hawk between October 10 and 30, 1911, making about 90 flights.

Models CH and G (1913) were hydroplanes, which were tested by Orville Wright at the Wright seaplane base on the Great Miami River (SL 6) and are described under that site. The Model G was designed by Wright Company engineer and factory manager Grover Loening, who later established his own company in New York City to manufacture airplanes of his design, including the Loening Amphibian and the Loening Monoplane.

Models E and F (1913) were land-based airplanes. The single-seat Model E, designed for exhibition flying, was one of two Wright models with a single pusher propeller rather than two propellers. The Model F was the first Wright model with a fuselage.

The Model H (1914) and the Model HS (1915) were military scout airplanes. The two-seat Model H had a 38-foot wing span and a six-foot chord (a line connecting the leading and trailing edges of the wing). The Model HS, a smaller version of the Model H, was the last Wright airplane to have a double vertical rudder or pusher-type propellers.

The Model K (1915) was the first Wright airplane to have tractor propellers (placed in front of the machine rather than behind), was equipped with pontoons and had a fuselage similar to the Model G flying boat.

The Model L (1916), the first Wright airplane with a single tractor propeller, was the last model manufactured by The Wright Company.

All of the Wright land-based models were tested at the Huffman Prairie flying field (EA 3).

In addition to manufacturing airplanes, The Wright Company managed an exhibition flying team in 1910 and 1911, described under CL 6, and manufactured airplane instruments and engines. Among the company's instruments was an incidence indicator that enabled the pilot to maintain a safe flying position, or angle of attack, thus preventing stalls and dives. The instrument sold for $50, weighed two and one-fourth pounds, had a dial that could be "read clearly at a distance of ten feet" and could be installed on a "convenient strut" of a biplane or "some member of the chassis" on a monoplane.

Most of The Wright Company engines were versions of their four-cylinder vertical model, of which about 100 were produced, or their later six-cylinder vertical model, of which about 50 were produced. The last engine produced by The Wright Company was a six-cylinder vertical model, a 60-horsepower in-line water-cooled motor called the Six-Sixty that sold for $1,875. A four-cylinder vertical type engine is on display at Carillon Historical Park (SL 1). A Six-Sixty is on display at the United States Air Force Museum (EA 1).

Orville Wright sold The Wright Company in October 1915 after obtaining controlling interest by buying out the other stockholders -- an action motivated by a desire to devote his time to research rather than to managing the company. Orville remained as a consultant to the new owners for a year, then set up the Wright Aeronautical Laboratory (WA 7) in 1916.

Orville sold The Wright Company to a group headed by William B. Thompson, Harry Payne Whitney and T. Frank Manville. About a year later, at the end of 1916, the company merged with the Glenn L. Martin Company to form the Wright-Martin Aircraft Company. In March 1917 the new company closed the former Wright Company factory and moved its operations out of town. Wright-Martin, reorganized as the Wright Aeronautical Corporation in 1919, produced airplane engines, including the Whirlwind, the first radial air-

The Wright Company factory buildings in 1911. These are now Buildings 1 and 2 at the GM Delphi Chassis Home Avenue Operations plant.

cooled engine. A Wright Whirlwind powered Charles A. Lindbergh's *Spirit of St. Louis* on his famous New York to Paris flight in 1927.

In 1929 Wright merged with the Curtiss Aeroplane Company to form the Curtiss-Wright Company. The Curtiss company originally was organized in 1909 by Glenn Curtiss, who had been the object of the Wright brothers' first patent infringement suit after Curtiss sold an airplane to the Aeronautical Society of New York for $7,500 in June 1909. The suit eventually was settled in the Wrights' favor in January 1914. (The Wrights initiated about 20 patent suits in America and Europe, all of which eventually were settled in their favor.) By the time of the merger, neither Curtiss nor Orville Wright was associated with the company that bore their names.

When first constructed in 1910 and 1911, The Wright Company factory buildings stood in the middle of a cornfield south of West Third Street along Coleman Avenue. (Coleman Avenue has since been incorporated into the General Motors property.) The one-story brick

Charles Taylor at work in The Wright Company factory. Taylor built the world's first airplane engine in the Wright brothers' bicycle shop at 1127 West Third Street in 1903.

Inland, the predecessor of the current plant, dates back to January 6, 1923, when General Motors formed the Inland Manufacturing Company, which was housed in the former Dayton Wright Plant 3 buildings. Inland's first product was a wood veneer-wrapped iron steering wheel for automobiles, adapted from a Dayton Wright airplane steering wheel designed by Harvey D. Geyer.

During World War II, Inland made an interesting contribution to the war effort with its Little Monster, an inexpensive (less than $2), light weight (slightly over a pound) pistol that "kicked like a mule." One million Little Monsters, each packaged with a Walt Disney cartoon showing how to operate it, were dropped over Europe for use by the Allied underground. Among other World War II contributions was a spark plug terminal seal, developed in cooperation with the Power Plant Laboratory at Wright Field (see EA 4), that solved an ignition problem encountered by American pilots when flying at high altitudes.

In 1989 Inland was merged into the Delco Products Division, which in turn evolved into the present-day Delphi Chassis Division, which includes the Home Avenue Operations plant. Today, the Home Avenue plant manufactures suspension parts for the automotive industry.

Building 1 of the former Wright Company factory is now the Union Work Center, with the Health and Safety Coordinator occupying the office once used by Orville Wright. Building 2 contains the Engineering Garage and Test Facility. A plaque commemorating the buildings' history was presented to Inland by Aviation, Trail, Inc. at a community dinner on September 15, 1983, in celebration of General Motors' 75th anniversary.

The Delphi Chassis Home Avenue Operations plant is not open to the public; however, the former Wright Company/Dayton Wright Airplane Company factory buildings can be viewed through the West Third Street entrance gate.

buildings, containing a total of 4,000 square feet and designed to resemble airplane hangars, have a distinctive curved roofline that at one time served as the Inland Manufacturing Company's logo. Three additional buildings of the same design, erected south of the two original buildings after Inland took over the property, are designated Buildings 3, 4 and 5.

The Wright Company Model L airplane, manufactured in 1916. This was the last model produced by The Wright Company.

Aviation Trail

1. The Old Court House

2. Wright Brothers Bicycle Shop Site

3. First Baptist Church of Dayton

4. The Engineers Club of Dayton

5. *The Dayton Journal* Newspaper Site

6. Centre City Building

7. Reibold Building

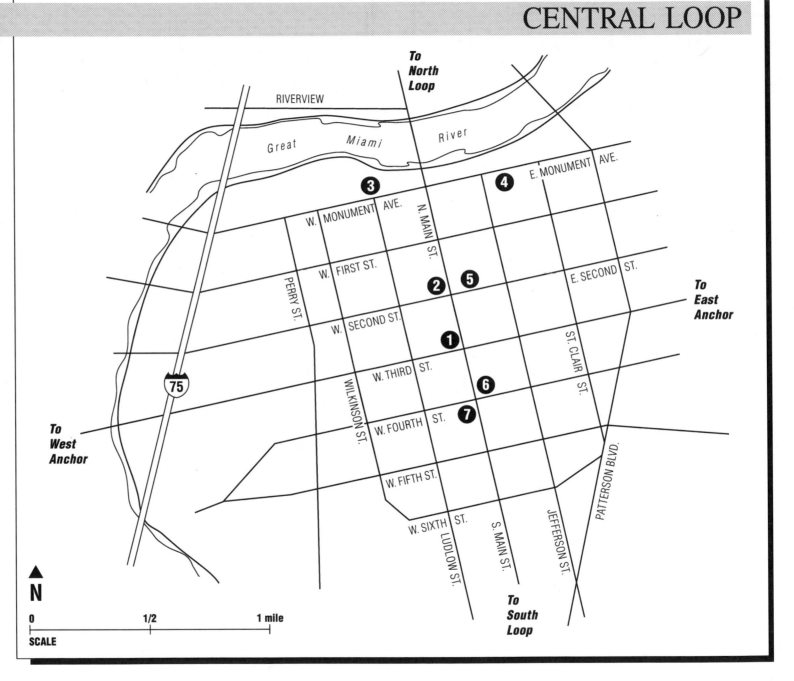

CENTRAL LOOP

The Aviation Trail Central Loop (CL), in downtown Dayton, probably is best covered as a walking tour.

Among Central Loop sites associated with the Wright brothers are:

- The site of a Wright bicycle shop,
- The church in which Orville's funeral was held,
- The office of the Wright exhibition flying team,
- An exhibit about the Wrights in The Old Court House,
- And The Engineers Club, with the original Wright engine number three.

Other sites include:

- The scene of early balloon ascensions,
- The site of *The Dayton Journal* newspaper office, which sponsored the first newspaper printed in the sky,
- And the unintended landing site of an early demonstration parachute jump.

CL 1   The Old Court House
7 North Main Street
Dayton, Ohio 45402

The Old Court House is the headquarters of the Montgomery County Historical Society. A museum on the first floor includes an exhibit about Wilbur and Orville Wright titled *The Wright Brothers, Men of Flight*. Among the items on display are an original desk from the Wright family home and the family *Bible*. The family consisted of Wilbur and Orville, their parents Milton and Susan, their brothers Reuchlin and Lorin and their sister Katharine.

Milton Wright, a bishop in the Church of the United Brethren in Christ, was born in a log cabin in Rush County, Indiana on November 17, 1828. Susan Catherine Koerner Wright was born at Hillsboro, Louden County, Virginia on April 30, 1831. Milton and Susan met in Hartsville, Indiana and were married on November 24, 1859. Susan died of tuberculosis at the family home on Hawthorn Street (WA 4) on July 4, 1889 at the age of 58. Milton, who never remarried, died in his sleep at the Wright mansion in the Dayton suburb of Oakwood, Hawthorn Hill (SL 11), on April 3, 1917 at the age of 88.

Although the world speaks of the Wright brothers as though there were only two, in actuality there were four: Wilbur and Orville and their two older brothers, Reuchlin and Lorin. Reuchlin was born on a farm near Fairmont, Indiana on March 17, 1861 and Lorin in Fayette County, Indiana on November 18, 1862. Reuchlin settled out west and died in Kansas City, Missouri on May 23, 1920 at the age of 59. Lorin remained in Dayton where he died on December 1, 1939 at the age of 77. Both Reuchlin and Lorin married and raised families.

Katharine is better known than Reuchlin and Lorin because she often travelled with Wilbur and Orville and acted as their hostess after they became famous. Katharine was born in the family home on Hawthorn Street on August 19, 1874. After graduation from Oberlin

The Wright family. Left to right: Wilbur, Katharine, Susan, Lorin, Milton, Reuchlin and Orville.

College in 1898, she became a teacher at Dayton's Steele High School. Late in life she married college classmate Henry J. Haskell on November 20, 1926 and moved to Kansas City, Missouri, where he was an editor of the *Kansas City Star*. Katharine died of pneumonia in Kansas City on March 3, 1929 at the age of 54.

Wilbur, named for Wilbur Fiske, a churchman his father admired, was born on a farm near Millville, Indiana on April 16, 1867. Orville, named for Unitarian minister Orville Dewey, a friend of his father, was born in the family's Hawthorn Street home on August 19, 1871, three years to the day before his sister Katharine. None of the five Wright children was given a middle name. Wilbur died of typhoid fever at the home on Hawthorn Street on May 30, 1912 at the age of 45. Orville died on January 30, 1948 at the age of 76, three days after suffering a heart attack at his laboratory on North Broadway Street (WA 6). Neither Wilbur nor Orville ever married.

Another exhibit in the Old Court House, titled *John H. Patterson: Innovator*, tells the story of the founder of the National Cash Register Company. A civic leader and donor to the city of Hills and Dales Park (SL 2), Patterson also was a strong supporter of local aviation activities. Patterson Field, now part of Wright-Patterson Air Force Base (EA 4), was named for John's nephew, Lieutenant Frank Stuart Patterson, who died in an airplane accident at Wilbur Wright Field (see EA 4) during World War 1.

The restored Old Court House, considered one of the finest examples of Greek Revival architecture in the United States, stands in an urban park setting on Courthouse Square. Completed in 1850, the building's features include a flying staircase in the rotunda, constructed by Jean Jacques Wuichet, a Swiss stonemason who came to Dayton in 1836 to help build the stone locks of the Miami and Erie Canal.

Museum hours are 10:00 a.m. to 4:30 p.m. Tuesday through Friday and 12:00 noon to 4:00 p.m. Saturday. Admission is free.

CL 2   Wright Brothers Bicycle Shop Site
23 West Second Street
Dayton, Ohio 45402

A Wright brothers bicycle shop was located at 23 West Second Street for about a year in 1895-1896, in a building that has since been demolished. The site is now occupied by part of a vacant department store building.

The West Second Street shop was unique in that it was the Wrights' only attempt to operate a shop in downtown Dayton. Except for the Exhibition Department of The Wright Company (CL 6), all of the Wrights' enterprises, including their job printing and airplane businesses, were located on the West Side, most within a few blocks of the family's Hawthorn Street home (WA 4). Even during the year they had the West Second Street shop, the brothers maintained a presence on the West Side with a second bicycle shop and a job printing business at 22 South Williams Street (WA 3).

At the time the Wright brothers opened their downtown shop the country was in the midst of the great bicycle boom of the 1890s, when approximately 400 American companies were turning out about 2,000,000 bicycles per year. Wilbur and Orville were not alone in trying to profit from the craze. In 1895 they faced competition from 12 other Dayton bicycle shops, including three across the street in the same block as theirs on West Second. By the following year the total had risen to 18, all located downtown except for the Wrights' West Side shop on South Williams.

The Wrights' downtown shop appears to have been a retail store perhaps combined with a repair service. Aside from a listing in the 1895-1896 *Dayton City Directory* and a brief note in their father's diary, dated May 24, 1895, little is known about the shop.

The Wrights' downtown bicycle shop was located in the east side of a three-story brick building whose owner, Nathan Mory, operated a money-lending business in the other half. In 1912 Rike's constructed a seven-story department store to the east of the building. Then two years later, the 11-story Miami Hotel was erected to the

Rike's Department Store around 1920. The Wright brothers had a bicycle shop in the three-story building behind Rike's in 1895-1896. The Miami Hotel is behind the former bicycle shop at the extreme left.

west, leaving the 23 West Second Street building plus two other small buildings sandwiched in between until they were demolished during a 1930s expansion of Rike's. Today, the entire north side of West Second Street from Main to Ludlow Streets is occupied by the closed department store, most recently occupied by Lazarus.

The store dates back to a store started by David L. Rike at 15-17 East Third Street in 1850. In 1893 the store moved to a new three-story (plus basement) building at Fourth and Main Streets, designed after a Worlds Fair building, where part of the Reibold Building (CL 7) now stands, then to its last location, at Second and Main, in 1912. In

1959 Rike's became part of Federated Department Stores, merging with Federated's Cincinnati Shillito's store in 1982 to form the Shillito Rike's division, later changed to Lazarus.

The Lazarus store was closed January 1, 1992 when the company decided to leave downtown in order to concentrate on its suburban stores. In 1995 Lazarus sold the vacant building to a group of local investors, who are now working with an international development company on a potential redevelopment plan for the property.

CL 3   First Baptist Church of Dayton
111 West Monument Avenue
Dayton, Ohio 45402

Orville Wright's funeral was held at the First Baptist Church on February 2, 1948. Orville died at Miami Valley Hospital at the age of 76 on January 30, three days after suffering a heart attack at his West Side laboratory (WA 6).

Orville's fatal heart attack was his second. His first, from which he appeared to have recovered, occurred the previous fall, on October 10, 1947, as he was hurrying up the steps of the National Cash Register Company to keep an appointment. During his recovery from that attack he was attended by Skippy Meyer, a Miami Valley Hospital nurse he greatly enjoyed teasing. When Skippy first entered his room upon his return to Miami Valley following his January attack, Orville reportedly greeted her with, "This is the only way I could find to see you again."

Orville's funeral service was conducted by Dr. Charles Lyon Seasholes, pastor of First Baptist Church. Although Orville was not a member of First Baptist (neither he nor Wilbur were church members after they became adults), he had expressed a desire that Dr. Seasholes perform the service, once remarking that as far as he was concerned there were only two ministers in Dayton, both Baptists, "one a colored minister on the West Side" and Dr. Seasholes. In his address at the

2:30 p.m. service, Dr. Seasholes said, "We are on hallowed ground today in this whole community where Orville Wright lived and worked and was our neighbor."

Friends, associates and dignitaries from across the country came to Dayton to attend the funeral. General Carl Spaatz, Commander of the United States Air Force, headed a delegation from Washington. Also attending were other military leaders, including nine generals and four admirals; industrialists, including Henry Ford II and Glenn L. Martin; businessmen, including Daytonians Charles F. Kettering and Edward A. Deeds (among the last to talk to Orville before he died); and former pupils and associates of Orville, including Walter Brookins, the first civilian taught to fly by the Wrights and a member of the Wright exhibition flying team (see CL 6), Grover Loening, an early factory manager of The Wright Company (WA 11), Charles Taylor, who made the first airplane engine in the Wrights' bicycle shop (WA 7), and Captain William J.Tate, at whose home Wilbur had stayed when he first arrived in Kitty Hawk, North Carolina in 1900. A loudspeaker system was installed to accommodate the large overflow crowd unable to find seating in the sanctuary.

Jet fighters from Wright-Patterson Air Force Base (EA 4) flew overhead as the funeral procession moved from the church to Woodland Cemetery (SL 12). Then they dipped their wings in salute at the graveside service as Orville was buried in the Wright family plot alongside his brother Wilbur, his sister Katharine and their parents.

Orville left an estate valued at $1,023,903, according to probate court records. Among his bequests were $300,000 to Oberlin College and annuities of $3,000 per year to his secretary Mabel Beck, $2,000 per year to the Wrights' long-time housekeeper Carrie Grumbach and $400 per year to Lottie (Charlotte) Jones, the family's laundress.

Wilbur Wright died of typhoid fever on May 30, 1912, almost 30 years before his brother Orville and less than nine years after the brothers invented the airplane. Wilbur's funeral was held on June 1, 1912 at the First Presbyterian Church, with Rev. E. Maurice Wilson officiating. The First Presbyterian Church, since demolished, stood on the northwest corner of West Second and North Ludlow Streets.

Wilbur's estate was estimated to be $277,000. Bequests included $1,000 to his father, Bishop Milton Wright; $50,000 each to his brothers Reuchlin and Lorin and sister Katharine; and the remainder (approximately $126,000) to Orville.

First Baptist Church was founded in 1837 as the First Regular Baptist Church by the remaining members after a schism had developed among the congregation of the original Dayton Baptist Church (formed in 1824). In 1915 First Baptist moved to its present location from a building at the corner of Main Street and Booher Lane that it had occupied since 1863. The impetus for building the new church on Monument Avenue came from the encroaching commercialism that followed construction of the nearby seven-story Rike's department store in 1912 -- and an offer of $125,000 for the church's strategically-located North Main Street property.

CL 4   The Engineers Club of Dayton
110 East Monument Avenue
Dayton, Ohio 45402

Orville Wright was a founding member and early president of The Engineers Club. The original Wright engine number three and other Wright memorabilia are on display in the clubhouse.

Engine number three, built in 1904 as an experimental model, was the last of the Wrights' horizontal-type engines. This engine has been called the grandfather of modern aviation power plants because it incorporated many of the principles used in subsequent airplane engines for years to come. Used mainly in stationary tests to improve performance and reliability, it was run continuously over long periods of time between 1904 and 1906. It was last used in 1907 when it powered the Wrights' first water-based machine, a hydrofoil, during tests on the Great Miami River near the Main Street bridge.

Wilbur and Orville Wright testing their hydrofoil on the Great Miami River by the Main Street bridge in 1907. The bridge, built in 1903 by H. E. Talbott, has since been replaced.

Circumstances forced the Wright brothers to invent the airplane engine as well as the airplane when they failed to find an established manufacturer able or willing to build an engine to their specifications. Experience in building engines to run the machinery in their bicycle shops helped them meet the challenge.

The Wrights already had reached many basic design decisions before beginning work on their first engine, the engine that powered their Flyer I. Among these were internal combustion for the power, as opposed to the steam engine, which was popular with earlier experimenters; a four-stroke cycle piston, instead of the two-stroke which had been favored previously; the use of water, rather than air, to cool the cylinders; the transmission of power to the propellers by chain drive instead of drive shafts or direct drive; and installing the engine with the cylinders in a horizontal position rather than vertical as was usual in automobiles of that time.

The Wright engine number one was built in 1903 in the brothers' bicycle shop on West Third Street (WA 7), with most of the parts machined on the shop's equipment by the Wrights' chief bicycle mechanic, Charley Taylor. The aluminum casting, a choice of material considered very innovative at the time, was made by a Dayton foundry. The engine had no fuel pump, using gravity instead. Horsepower ranged from 12 to 16. The reassembled engine number one is on display in the restored Flyer I at the Smithsonian Institution in Washington, D. C.

The Wright engine number two, built in 1904, powered the Wrights' Flyer II in tests at Huffman Prairie (EA 3) from May 26 to December 9, 1904 and, after modifications, their Flyer III in tests from June 23 to October 16, 1905. The horsepower of this engine ranged from 15 to 21. Improvements included a fuel pump and a manually-operated cylinder compression release device to hold the exhaust valves open. Engine number two is on display in the restored Flyer III at Carillon Historical Park (SL 1).

With engine number three, the Wrights attained approximately 25 horsepower, about twice that of their first engine although the two engines were about equal in size. New features included holes around the cylinders that served as exhaust ports when they were uncovered

Orville Wright, left, and Charles F. Kettering at The Engineers Club in 1942.

by the pistons at the end of a stroke. Bequeathed to The Engineers Club by Orville Wright, engine number three was dedicated as an exhibit on February 1, 1949.

The Engineers Club was founded in 1914 by industrialist Edward A. Deeds and inventor Charles F. Kettering, organizers of the Dayton Wright Airplane Company (SL 5). In founding the club, Deeds and Kettering envisioned a place where local inventors could get together to discuss their ideas. A stated aim of the club was "the making of a technical city where creative endeavor finds reward." They built the clubhouse, dedicated in 1918, and personally underwrote all expenses until it became self-supporting in 1924.

Deeds and Kettering alternated the office of president between them from 1914 to 1923. Charles H. Paul was the third president (1923-1924), Orville Wright the fourth (1924-1925) and W. A. Chryst (1925-1926) the fifth. Paul came to Dayton as an engineer for the Miami Conservancy District, the flood control project established after the disastrous 1913 flood, and helped establish the original privately-owned airport at what is now Dayton International Airport (NL 11). Chryst was an early associate of Deeds and Kettering in the Barn Gang, a group who worked on early automobile inventions, including the self-starter, in the barn behind Deeds' house. The restored barn is an exhibit at the Kettering-Moraine Museum (SL 4).

Located along the Great Miami River across Monument Avenue from the club is Van Cleve Park, which commemorates the landing of Dayton's first settlers on April 1, 1796 at the foot of present-day St. Clair Street. Among those in the first boat to arrive after an 11-day trip up the Great Miami River from Cincinnati was Catharine Van Cleve Thompson, Wilbur and Orville Wright's great-great-grandmother. Their Van Cleve model bicycle was named for Catharine, the first white woman to set foot in Dayton.

The Engineers Club is a private club; however, it welcomes visitors. To arrange a tour, telephone the club office at 937-228-2148.

CL 5 *The Dayton Journal* Newspaper Site
15 East Second Street
Dayton, Ohio 45402

The first newspaper printed in the sky was published on June 29, 1909 by *The Dayton Journal*, then located in a building at 15 East Second Street that has since been demolished.

Published in celebration of the paper's 101st anniversary, the Sky Edition was printed on a 52-pound hand press carried aloft in a balloon, the *Hoosier*, piloted by the balloon's owner, L. G. Brumbaugh, of Indianapolis, Indiana. Harold L. Burba, later the paper's managing editor, acted as pressman. Also on board were George A. McClelland, the paper's editor and publisher; Dayton balloonists Luzern Custer (see CL 7) and Dr. Pliney M. Crume; and Frank G. Carley and B. H. Wendler, who were associated with the Dayton Dental Supply Company.

Inflated with $80 worth of illuminating gas from the Dayton Power and Light Company, the balloon took off from Buck Island, a man-made island in the Great Miami River near the foot of St. Clair Street. (Buck Island was dredged out by the Miami Conservancy District as part of the flood control project initiated after the 1913 Dayton flood.)

Three editions of the paper were printed and distributed during the six hour flight, which covered 104 miles before the *Hoosier* landed on a farm south of Indianapolis. The second edition contained this lead story:

> AT 11 40 WE ARE 6700 FEET HIGH WE
> ARE PASSING FRANKLIN
>   GOING Southwest,
>   Taking Dinner, Speed 26 Miles,
>   1 O'clock Shot at by farmer - He missed

Six years earlier *The Dayton Journal* lost an opportunity to be the first to print the story of the world's first man-carrying powered flight when one of its editors failed to realize the importance of the event.

After the Wright brothers completed the first successful tests of their Flyer on December 17, 1903 at Kitty Hawk, North Carolina, Orville sent his father in Dayton the following telegram:

> Success four flights thursday morning all against twenty one mile wind started from Level with engine power alone average speed through air thirty one miles longest 57 seconds inform Press home xxxx Christmas. Orevelle Wright 525P

(In the transmission, 59 seconds became 57 and Orville's name was misspelled.)

When Bishop Wright received the message at 5:25 that evening, he asked his son Lorin to inform the press as requested. Lorin sought out Frank Tunison, the *Journal*'s telegraph editor who was also the Associated Press representative in Dayton, to report the historic event. However, Tunison was disinterested. "Fifty-seven sec-onds, hey.?" he said, "If it had been 57 minutes then it might have been a news item."

Although the Wright brothers had hoped to give Dayton the honor of announcing the news of their success, it turned out that the first report appeared in the Norfolk *Virginia Pilot* on the morning of December 18. The reporter, H. P. Moore, obtained the story from the Norfolk telegraph operator, and wrote the article almost totally from imagination since he had been unable to interview any eyewitnesses.

Moore's article apparently was the basis for the story in that day's *Dayton Evening Herald*, the first news of the Wrights' accom-plishment to appear in their home town. Headlined "Dayton Boys Fly Airship," the front page story named Wilbur as the operator of the machine, described as having one six-bladed propeller beneath the engine and another extending horizontally to the rear. And the flight was said to have covered three miles. A second article, datelined Day-ton, quoted the telegram received by Bishop Wright.

In 1949 *The Journal* was merged with *The Herald* to form the lone Dayton morning newspaper, *The Journal Herald*, after the two papers were purchased by James M. Cox, publisher of the *Dayton Daily News*, the lone evening newspaper. In 1986 *The Journal Herald* was merged into the *Dayton Daily News*, which then became the Day-ton area's lone daily newspaper, putting out only a morning edition.

The 15 East Second Street building in which *The Dayton Jour-nal* was once located was demolished in 1988 to make way for the new Citizens Federal Centre office building.

CL 6   Centre City Building
        40 South Main Street
        Dayton, Ohio 45402

The Centre City Building, originally named the United Brethren (U. B.) Building, once housed the office of the Wright exhibition flying team and later was the scene of an unintended parachute landing by Lawrence Sperry, Sr.

The Wright Company Exhibition Department occupied room 1310 from March 1910 to November 1911 in what was then called the U. B. Building. The department was established shortly after Wilbur and Orville Wright formed The Wright Company (WA 10) because the brothers thought flying demonstrations would be more profitable than manufacturing airplanes -- at least until a market for the new machine had been developed. The team was disbanded when the company switched its emphasis to airplane production with the completion of its second factory building (WA 11) in November 1911.

Roy Knabenshue, a dirigible pilot from Toledo, Ohio with exhibition flying and promotion experience, was hired as manager of the team and Mabel Beck, as Knabenshue's secretary. (Mabel Beck later became Wilbur Wright's secretary until his death in 1912, and Orville's until his death in 1948.) Initial members of the flying team included Walter R. Brookins, a former student of Katharine Wright; Duval La Chapelle, a French mechanic who had worked for Wilbur Wright in France; Ralph Johnstone, a trick bicycle rider and circus clown whom Knabenshue had discovered out West; Arch Hoxsey, an auto racer and friend of Knabenshue; and Frank Coffyn, whose father, a New York banker, was a friend of some of the company's stockholders.

The team's initial training was at a flying field near Montgomery, Alabama, now part of Maxwell Air Force Base. The site was chosen by Wilbur because of incentives offered by the local Commerce Club: free use of the field, which he selected; a hangar constructed at no cost to the company; and free transportation for the students to and from Montgomery. Orville arrived near the end of March to begin the training.

Several members of The Wright Company exhibition flying team at Huffman Prairie in 1910. Left to right: Frank Coffyn, Ralph Johnstone, James Davis, Orville Wright, A. L. Welsh and Duval La Chapelle.

The first to learn to fly was Brookins, the Wrights' first civilian student. Brookins then trained Hoxsey. La Chapelle, Johnstone and Coffyn learned to fly at Huffman Prairie (EA 3) after the Alabama field was closed in May 1910, just two months after it opened. A disadvantage of the southern location stemmed from the need for frequent repairs to the airplane, which could be made more easily if the training site were located closer to the factory in Dayton.

The team's first exhibition was at Indianapolis, Indiana on June 13 to 18, 1910. Other engagements included the first recorded public night flights, at Asbury Park, New Jersey on August 19, 1910; a flight on September 29, 1910 sponsored by the *Chicago Record Herald* in which Brookins set a cross-country record of 187 miles in about seven hours elapsed time; and participation in the International Aviation Tournament at Belmont Park, New York from October 22 to 30, 1910.

Unfortunately, two members of the original team were killed during the first year. Johnstone died in a crash at Overland Park, Denver, Colorado on November 17 and Hoxsey was killed in a flying accident at Los Angeles, California on December 31.

As anticipated by the Wrights, the exhibition flying team did indeed prove profitable. The Wright Company charged a $1,000 per day fee for each pilot who participated in an event. The pilots were paid $20 per week plus $50 per day for each day they flew. The company's gross income from the exhibition department was about $1,000,000 per year.

Roy Knabenshue (1876-1960) was inducted into the National Aviation Hall of Fame (see EA 1) in 1965.

Lawrence Sperry, Sr. made his unintended landing on the 11th floor ledge of the U. B. Building while demonstrating a parachute of his design at McCook Field (NL 1) in September 1918.

Sperry was the son of Elmer A. Sperry, head of the Sperry Gyroscope Company, who was known as the "gyroscope man" after the gyroscopes for seagoing vessels produced by his company. At one time, before his marriage to movie star Winifred Allen, Lawrence shared a house in Massapequa, New York with Grover Loening, an early factory manager of The Wright Company (see WA 11, SL 6).

Lawrence Sperry first became interested in parachute design while serving in the Navy during World War I. At that time the only parachutes in use were cumbersome and unreliable types stored in or under the fuselage of the airplane. Lawrence was convinced that a better design would be a parachute attached to the airman, which the user could open manually after he had cleared the aircraft. The McCook Field jump was to be the first demonstration of a parachute Lawrence designed based on these principles. The occasion was a series of tests being conducted by the Naval Consulting Board, of which his father was a member.

The McCook Field test became a tug-of-war between father and son. The elder Sperry had forbidden his son to conduct the demonstration himself because Lawrence had been grounded as a result of injuries suffered in an aerial torpedo experiment several months earlier. To insure his ban held, Elmer had hidden his son's parachute.

The U. B. Building before the 1924 enlargement.

On the other hand, Lawrence was equally determined that no one but he should make the jump. Lawrence eventually won the test of wills by discovering the parachute's hiding place and by enlisting the aid of McCook test pilot Lieutenant John Reddy. At the scheduled time for the demonstration, the two retrieved the parachute and took off in a LePere powered by a Liberty engine. Then Lawrence made a beautiful jump just north of the field.

Lawrence's troubles began when a sudden gust of wind caught his parachute shortly after it opened. Instead of landing at McCook as he had intended, a change in the wind pushed him south of the field across the Great Miami River into downtown Dayton. There he drifted helplessly down Main Street, followed by a crowd of onlookers and a fire engine sent to aid in his rescue, until his parachute snagged on a cornice of the U. B. Building, stranding him 11 floors above the ground.

As the firemen rushed to the roof to assist him, Lawrence calmly pulled himself up to a one-foot ledge by the shrouds of his parachute, then worked his way over to a corner of the building and floated down to the street, landing unhurt in the firemen's net.

Lawrence Sperry was the inventor of a number of airplane instruments, including an automatic stabilizer based on principles employed by his father in the manufacture of marine gyroscopes. He also developed the Sperry Messenger, the first American sports plane, and was the contractor for the Army's Verville-Sperry Messenger, a monoplane designed by Alfred Verville at McCook Field. Sperry died on December 13, 1923 at the age of 30 when his airplane went down in the icy waters of the English Channel as he attempted to fly from England to the Netherlands.

Lawrence Sperry, Sr. (1892-1923) was inducted into the National Aviation Hall of Fame (see EA 1) in 1981. His father, Elmer A. Sperry (1860-1930), was inducted into the National Aviation Hall of Fame in 1973.

The Centre City Building dates back to 1834 when a four-story structure was erected on the northeast corner of Fourth and Main Streets by the United Brethren Printing Establishment. Later additions included a 14-story office tower added in 1904 and an enlargement in 1924 that made the building the largest concrete structure in the world at that time.

Today the 21-story Centre City Building contains commercial space on the first floor, various offices on the floors above, and a penthouse on the top floors of the tower, now the home of the building's owner.

CL 7   Reibold Building
117 South Main Street
Dayton, Ohio 45402

The Reibold Building was the site of an early record-breaking balloon flight and of an amusing incident associated with the first non-stop flight across the continent. The balloon pilot on both occasions was Luzern Custer, a Dayton inventor and manufacturer.

The record-breaking flight occurred in 1909 when Custer ascended from the top of the ten-story building and landed one hour later in Middletown, Ohio, about 20 miles away -- the longest distance covered by a balloon in one hour up to that time.

The amusing incident occurred on May 2, 1923 when Custer again ascended from the top of the Reibold building, this time in an unsuccessful attempt to welcome two McCook Field (NL 1) test pilots as they flew over Dayton on the first nonstop flight across the continent. Appointed by the Kiwanis Club to arrange a suitable welcome for the local flyers, Custer decided to greet them in his balloon trailing a "Welcome" sign. Notes made by Custer at the time detail some of the problems he encountered.

To begin with, Custer admitted he carried 40 cylinders of hydrogen with which to inflate his 500-cubic foot balloon up to the top of the building in a passenger elevator -- without a permit and with passengers on board. Then he took off from the wrong side of the building according to the prevailing wind and became tangled in some guy wires and a smokestack and almost landed on an outhouse behind the Young Women's League, next door to the Reibold Building on Fourth Street.

Eventually Custer became airborne, but his troubles were not over. At Miller's Ford, north of Dayton, he barely missed crashing into a fast-moving freight train after being caught in a downdraft and the more he waved, the more the engineer blew his whistle. Finally he landed in a cornfield where the spectators who had been following his flight trampled the farmer's corn.

Custer suggested some of his troubles might have been avoided had he used sand as ballast instead of using a hand-operated propeller to move the balloon up and down. His notes ended, "Never did see Kelly or Macready!"

Custer's ballooning activities earned him membership in the Early Birds, an organization of pilots who flew a gas balloon, glider or airplane before December 17, 1916. His business activities earned him a national reputation as a manufacturer of amusement park rides, such as the Custer Car, a miniature automobile, and personal transportation equipment, such as the Custer Buckboard, used at golf courses and airports. Examples of his transportation products are at Carillon Historical Park (SL 1). Luzern Custer died in 1962 at the age of 74.

The two McCook pilots Custer attempted to greet in 1923 were Lieutenants John A. Macready and Oakley G. Kelly. Their cross-country flight was made in a Fokker F-IV, an open cockpit, single engine monoplane manufactured in the Netherlands and purchased by the United States Air Service for $30,000. Designated Air Service T-2 (the "T" stood for transport), the machine was specially modified at McCook Field for the historic flight. Among the modifications were the installation of a Liberty V-12 engine, and the addition of a 410-gallon fuel tank between the spars of the wing center section and an 185-gallon fuel tank in the cabin.

The May 2-3, 1923 flight was the third attempt by Macready and Kelly to fly nonstop across the continent. This time, instead of flying west to east as in their first two attempts, they flew in the opposite direction, taking off from Roosevelt Field, Long Island, New York at 12:36 p.m. on May 2. They landed at Rockwell Field, San Diego, California at 3:26 p.m. (EST) on May 3, after covering 2,470 miles in 26 hours and 50 minutes with only a Rand-McNally road map to guide them.

By demonstrating the practicability of commercial aviation and providing data in support of an increased role for the airplane in national defense, this pioneer flight laid the groundwork for further development of civil and military applications of the airplane. By 1926 the first commercial airmail flights had begun; by 1930 the first airline stewardesses had been hired; by 1936 more than 2,300 airports had been established in the U. S. and by 1940 airplanes were proving to be a deciding factor in World War II.

The Young Women's League on Fourth Street. The rear of the Reibold Building, site of two of Luzern Custer's balloon ascensions, is visible in the upper left corner.

The Reibold Building once housed the Elder-Johnson department store, predecessor of the present day Elder-Beerman department store chain. The building is now owned by Montgomery County, which uses it as office space, with some commercial space on the first floor.

Aviation Trail

1. Carillon Historical Park

2. Hills and Dales Park

3. Moraine Farm

4. Kettering-Moraine Museum

5. Former Dayton Wright Airplane Company Main Plant

6. Wright Seaplane Base

7. Pinnacle Hill

8. Wright B Flyer Hanger

9. International Women's Air and Space Museum

10. Wright Memorial Library

11. Hawthorn Hill

12. Woodland Cemetery

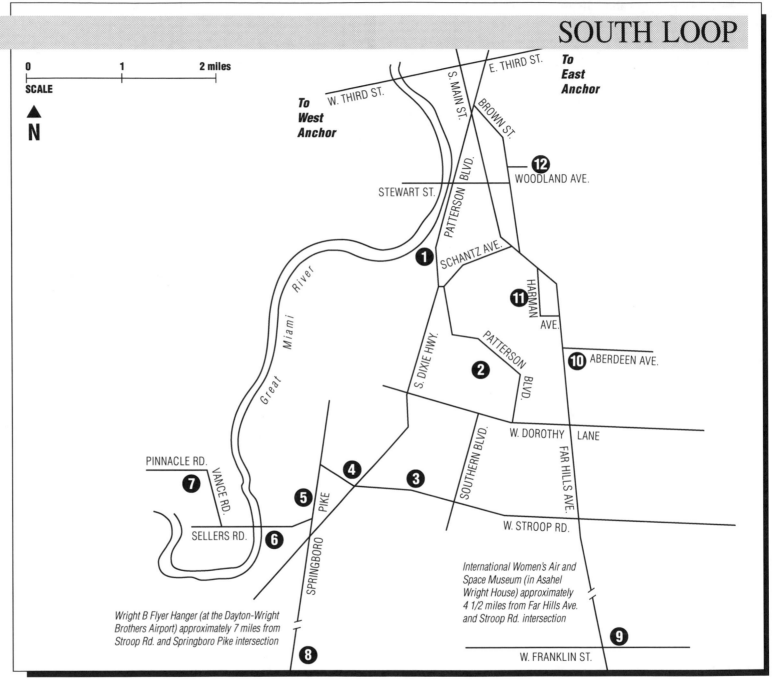

Wright B Flyer Hanger (at the Dayton-Wright Brothers Airport) approximately 7 miles from Stroop Rd. and Springboro Pike intersection

International Women's Air and Space Museum (in Asahel Wright House) approximately 4 1/2 miles from Far Hills Ave. and Stroop Rd. intersection

SOUTH LOOP

The Aviation Trail South Loop (SL) covers sites in south Dayton, the Dayton suburbs of Kettering, Moraine, Centerville and Oakwood, and Miami Township.

South Loop sites related to the Wright Brothers include:
- Pinnacle Hill, where the brothers observed the flight of birds,
- The Wright Seaplane Base on the Great Miami River, where Orville tested Wright Company hydroplanes,
- *Hawthorn Hill*, the Wright mansion in Oakwood,
- The Kettering-Moraine Museum, whose Wright brothers exhibit includes original furniture from *Hawthorn Hill*,
- Carillon Historical Park, with the original Wright Flyer III and a replica of the bicycle shop in which the Wrights built the world's first successful airplane,
- A look-alike, flyable Wright Model B airplane constructed by a group of local aviation enthusiasts,
- And the Wright Memorial Library in Oakwood, where Orville served as a member of the Board.

Sites related to industrialist Edward A. Deeds and inventor Charles F. Kettering and the Dayton Wright Airplane Company they formed include:
- The Dayton Wright Experimental Station at Deeds' estate, *Moraine Farm*,
- And the Dayton Wright Main Plant at what is now a General Motors engine plant.

Other South Loop sites are:
- The landing site of the first night emergency freefall parachute jump,
- The International Women's Air and Space Museum, in the Asahel Wright House, the restored Centerville home of the Wright brothers' great-uncle,
- And Woodland Cemetery, where the Wrights and others mentioned in *A Field Guide to Flight* are buried.

SL 1 Carillon Historical Park
2001 South Patterson Boulevard
Dayton, Ohio 45409

Carillon Historical Park is an outdoor museum depicting the history of the Miami Valley. Among its exhibits are a replica of the Wright brothers' last bicycle shop (WA 7) and Wright Hall, which houses the original Wright Flyer III.

The Flyer III, built in 1905, was the world's first practical airplane and the one in which the Wright brothers said they "really learned to fly." After being modified in 1908, the Flyer III also was the airplane in which the Wrights carried a passenger for the first time.

Not content merely to be the first in the sky when they flew their Flyer I at Kitty Hawk, North Carolina on December 17, 1903, Wilbur and Orville Wright continued to advance the state of the art of aeronautics by building two more experimental machines: the Flyer II, tested at Huffman Prairie (EA 3) in 1904, and the Flyer III, tested in 1905. By the end of the 1905 season, the Wrights not only had learned how to fly but had demonstrated that the airplane was a practical invention.

From the beginning, the Wright brothers realized that learning to pilot an airplane was just as crucial to manned flight as the four problems they had solved in building the Flyer I: how to control the airplane, how to obtain lift, how to provide power and how to convert that power into thrust.

Wilbur once said, " . . . if you really wish to learn (about flying) you must mount a machine and become acquainted with its tricks by actual trial." Interestingly, in addition to "mounting the machine," the Wrights also made frequent use of the technique of visualization in learning to become skilled pilots. Grover Loening, an early manager of The Wright Company (WA 11), attributed much of the brothers' success to their practice of "mental flying," reporting how "Orville would spend hours in a hangar seated in a plane imagining all kinds of flight difficulties. Then he would make the proper moves to offset

A restored Wright brothers bicycle, now on display at the Wright bicycle shop replica at Carillon Historical Park. Although the nameplate is missing, papers accompanying the bicycle indicate it is an original Van Cleve Model.

them. He must have flown thousands of miles (in his mind) in his efforts to perfect himself as a pilot."

The Flyer III was a vast improvement over the Flyer I in maneuverability and in distance covered. Instead of the straight-line flights of Flyer I, the Flyer III could bank, turn, circle and make figure eights. The improvement in distance was equally dramatic. The longest of the four flights made by the Flyer I was 852 feet in 59 seconds. The longest of the 50 flights made by the Flyer III between June 23 and October 16, 1905 was more than 24 miles in just under 40 minutes.

The Flyer III was the last of the Wrights' three experimental airplanes; that is, the last before they began giving public demonstrations of their invention in 1908. All three were biplanes (two wings, one above the other) with two pusher propellers mounted in the rear and a pair of landing skids. The pilot flew the airplane lying prone

The Wright Flyer III at Huffman Prairie, September 7, 1905. The restored Flyer III is at Carillon Historical Park.

with his hips resting in a leather cradle attached to part of the control mechanism. The airplane was controlled by sideway movements of the pilot's body in the leather cradle and through a hand lever.

The Flyer I, flown on the sand dunes at Kitty Hawk, was launched by means of a trolley running along a 60-foot monorail. The airplane's skids rested on the wheeled trolley as it rolled along the rail until the machine attained enough speed to become airborne. The machine was eight feet high and 21 feet long, had a 40-foot four-inch wing span and weighed 750 pounds loaded. A 12-horsepower Wright engine powered the two spruce propellers. The spruce and ash airframe was covered with *Pride of the West* unbleached muslin. According to Orville, the plane carried 63 pounds per horsepower at a speed of 30 miles per hour. After four flights on December 17, 1903, the Flyer I was damaged by a gust of wind and never flown again. The reconstructed Flyer I is on display at the Smithsonian Institution in Washington, D. C.

The Flyer II made 105 flights at Huffman Prairie between May 26 and December 9, 1904. During this season, the Wrights devised a new launching technique using a derrick and weight (also called a catapult) to provide additional momentum as the machine rolled down the starting track. Also that season Wilbur flew the first complete circle ever made in an airplane. Similar in dimensions to the Flyer I, the second Wright airplane was powered by a 16-horsepower Wright engine. At the end of the season, the Wrights dismantled the airplane and used some of its parts, including the engine, to construct the Flyer III.

As flown in 1905, the Flyer III was eight feet high and 28 feet long. It had a 40-foot six-inch wing span, a takeoff weight of 855 pounds and a speed of 35 miles per hour. A 20-horsepower engine powered the two spruce propellers. The spruce and ash airframe was covered with bleached cotton. Longer booms to the forward elevator and to the rudder increased the plane's longitudinal and directional control. As exhibited at Carillon Historical Park, the Flyer III has been restored to its 1905 configuration and equipped with the original Wright engine number two, a four-cylinder horizontal model.

The Flyer III was put in storage at the end of the 1905 season and the Wrights did no more flying for almost two and one-half years while they waited for approval of their patent applications and sought arrangements to market their invention.

After receiving a contract from the United States Army, the Wrights modified the Flyer III to conform to the contract's specifications, then made 22 flights at Kitty Hawk from May 6 to 14, 1908 to regain their flying skills. On the last day, Charles W. Furnas, a Wright mechanic from Dayton, became their first passenger.

The 1908 version of the Flyer III could carry two people, both sitting upright. The machine also had a new control system and a new 35-horsepower engine with vertical cylinders instead of horizontal as in the previous Wright motors. The Flyer III was wrecked in an accident on the last day of the Kitty Hawk flights.

The 1908 version of the Flyer III was similar to the Wright Model A, the plane purchased by the United States Army in 1909 and redesignated Signal Corps Airplane No. 1. The Model A was eight feet one inch high and 28 feet 11 inches long. It had a 26-foot six-inch wing span, a 1,200 pound takeoff weight and a speed of 44 miles per hour. A 30-horsepower Wright engine powered the two spruce pusher propellers. The spruce and ash airframe was covered with unbleached muslin. A reproduction of the Signal Corps Airplane No. 1 is on display at the United States Air Force museum (EA 1).

Foreign versions of the Model A included a French-produced Wright airplane piloted by British aviator C. S. Rolls in a flight across the English Channel on June 2, 1910.

The Wright Flyer III airplane at Carillon Historical Park was reconstructed under the direction of Orville Wright and is exhibited in a building designed so the viewer can look down on the machine instead of up, as suggested by Orville. The Flyer III is a National Historic Landmark.

Wright Hall and its Flyer III exhibit are one of the four scattered sites in the Dayton Aviation Heritage National Historical Park (see WA 3).

A replica of the bicycle shop in which Wilbur and Orville Wright built the first airplane is next to Wright Hall. (The original building is an exhibit at Greenfield Village in Dearborn, Michigan.)

The airplane was built in the shed at the rear, which was equipped as a machine shop similar to the one in the park's replica. The bicycle shop also has an exhibit about the Wright brothers' printing business.

Carillon Historical Park was established in 1942 as a gift to the community by Colonel Edward A. Deeds, National Cash Register Company executive and a founder of the Dayton Wright Airplane Company (SL 5). Deeds also provided an endowment for the park's maintenance. The park is named for the carillon tower that dominates the park's green space -- a project of Deeds' wife Edith, a well-known local musician. The carillon's original 40 bells were replaced with 50 mechanically-operated bells in 1988; seven more were added in 1995.

The exhibit portion of the 65-acre park includes more than 25 buildings related to the history of the Dayton area. The park is owned and operated by the nonprofit Carillon Historical Park, Inc..

The park is open May 1 through October 31. Exhibit hours are 10:00 a.m. to 6:00 p.m. Tuesday through Saturday and 1:00 to 6:00 p.m. Sunday from May to August and 10:00 a.m. to 5.00 p.m. Tuesday through Saturday and 1:00 to 5:00 p.m. Sunday in September and October. Admission is $2.00 for adults, $1.00 ages 6 to 17 and under 6 free.

SL 2. Hills and Dales Park
Patterson Boulevard
Kettering, Ohio 45409

The first night emergency freefall parachute jump was made by McCook Field test pilot Lieutenant John A. Macready on July 18, 1924. Macready landed unhurt at the edge of a deep ravine near the Dayton Community Country Club golf course at Hills and Dales Park. His airplane crashed in flames in a field near Lebanon Pike, now called Far Hills Avenue.

On the night of his historic jump, Macready was returning from a routine flight to Columbus, Ohio when at about 10:00 p.m. the engine of his DeHaviland-4 died as he approached McCook Field (NL 1) at 5,000 feet. Hesitant to attempt a glide into McCook, which was located in a populous area near downtown Dayton, Macready headed south toward the open area of the golf course. But before he could reach the golf course and a safe landing, the plane's propellers suddenly stopped, forcing him to bail out.

As his plane plunged through the darkness (by now at 3,000 feet), Macready put a flashlight in his pocket, tossed out two flares (the first of which failed), then heading his plane out of the way of his parachute, "leaped into the inky space," as he later described his experience. As he floated to the ground, he called out, "Hello below! Hello down there!" to attract assistance should he be injured in landing.

At that very moment, the C. E. Ainsworths and the Ed Wuichets were sitting on the lawn of the Ainsworth estate on Meadow Lane in what was then called Short Hills. Noticing Macready's flare lighting up the sky, Ed Wuichet remarked, "Look at that meteor!" shortly before they heard Macready's call. Realizing his mistake, Wuichet called back, "Where are you?" to which the airman replied, "Up here in a parachute," just before landing in a woods on the edge of a 90-foot ravine where his parachute became tangled in the trees. The Ainsworths and the Wuichets quickly rescued the pilot; then all five took off in the Ainsworth automobile in search of Macready's plane. They soon found it in a wheat field about 200 feet from Lebanon Pike, surrounded by a crowd of several hundred people who were concerned about the pilot, whom they supposed to be trapped in the burning wreckage. Macready reported for work as usual at 8:00 the next morning.

In his years at McCook, Macready participated in several other firsts and set a number of records. Among the firsts were the first nonstop flight across the continent, in 1923, which is described under CL 7, and the first aerial photographic survey of the United States, in 1924. On the survey, Macready and McCook pilot Lieutenant A. W. Stevens flew over 10,000 miles and took more than 2,000 photographs in a prelude to today's aerial mapping. Macready's many records included a high altitude record of 37,888 feet, which he set on

McCook Field test pilot Lieutenant John A. Macready in 1924.

September 28, 1921 while circling Dayton for 47 minutes in a two-seat LePere biplane with a Liberty engine during a routine super-charger test. In 1924 Macready wrote, "It is lonely work fighting the elements at the earth's ceiling." John A. Macready (1887-1979) was inducted into the National Aviation Hall of Fame (see EA 1) in 1968.

Macready's flight on the night of his historic parachute jump was part of an experiment in which a McCook pilot made a round trip flight between Dayton and Columbus every night to test the country's first lighted airway (see NL 1).

Hills and Dales Park, established in 1911 as a recreation area for National Cash Register Company (NCR) employees, was donated to the community in 1918 by John H. Patterson, a founder of the company. A statue of Patterson mounted on his horse stands on a hill along Patterson Boulevard, overlooking the park's Dayton Community Country Club golf course. The hill provides an excellent view of several of the area's numerous ridges, which are described under SL 7. Patterson, a pioneer in modern business management, introduced many of the employee relations and sales techniques that underlie current management theory. The Old Court House Museum (CL 1) has an exhibit about Patterson's NCR career.

Patterson Boulevard is named for John H. Patterson. Dorothy Lane is named for a path along which his daughter Dorothy once rode her pony. Far Hills Avenue is named for Patterson's estate, *The Far Hills*, which was replaced in 1924 by a house built by his son Frederick (now the Lutheran Church of Our Savior, 155 East Thruston Boulevard). Patterson Field, now part of Wright-Patterson Air Force Base (EA 4), was named for Lieutenant Frank S. Patterson, son of John's brother Frank.

Today, the 294-acre Hills and Dales Park includes two 18-hole golf courses, hiking trails, picnic areas with shelterhouses and the Michael Solomon Pavilion.

The park is open from 8:00 a.m. to 10:00 p.m.

SL 3   *Moraine Farm*
1233 West Stroop Road
Kettering, Ohio 45429

South Field, the private airfield of Colonel Edward A. Deeds at his estate, *Moraine Farm*, once served as the Experimental Station of the Dayton Wright Airplane Company, formed in 1917 by Deeds and Charles F. Kettering to manufacture warplanes for World War I. The Experimental Station, located to the east of Dayton Wright's main plant (SL 5), was the company's research and development section.

The first guided missile, the *Bug*, developed under the direction of Charles F. Kettering at the Dayton Wright Airplane Company Experimental Station in 1918. From the original glass negative.

Among the station's projects were a number of firsts, including the development of the first guided missile.

The first guided missile, called the *Bug*, was developed in 1918 under the direction of Kettering, a Dayton inventor who headed the Experimental Station. A predecessor of the German World War II buzz bomb, the *Bug* was a small robot biplane designed to act as an aerial torpedo, using the analogy of an ocean of air. Specifications called for the cost of one firing not to exceed the cost of firing one eight-inch shell from the German Big Bertha (a large cannon) and for an accuracy of at least half that of the big gun.

As developed under Kettering, the *Bug* was a simple, cheap and expendable weapon. The robot plane was 12 feet six inches long

Aerial view of Edward A. Deeds' estate, *Moraine Farm*. Deeds' 1928 Ford tri-motor airplane is parked at the landing pad on his private airfield to the left of his residence.

plunging the explosive-laden body to the earth. The missile could be easily assembled in the field with a single tool, a combination screwdriver and wrench. And it was easily launched from a carriage rolled along a moveable track headed into the prevailing wind.

By the end of World War I less than 50 *Bugs* had been completed out of an order for 40,000, none of which was used in combat because, as it turned out, all the European targets were beyond its range. A replica of the *Bug* is on display at the United States Air Force Museum (EA 1).

Local aviation folklore includes a story about an early test of the *Bug*, a top secret military project. Upon being launched during this particular experiment, instead of landing at the South Field Experimental Station as planned, the robot plane unexpectedly took off to the east, flying rapidly out of sight. After half an hour of uncertainty, the worried South Field team received a call from Wilbur Wright Field (see EA 4) reporting that the *Bug* had been sighted headed toward Xenia, at which news the South Field group immediately leaped into an automobile in frantic pursuit of the secret weapon. A short distance out of Xenia they encountered a farmer who reported he had seen a plane crash but he had failed to find the pilot. To this a quick-thinking team member replied that the pilot had parachuted out and had already been taken to a hospital, thus maintaining the project's secrecy.

Deeds disassociated himself from Dayton Wright shortly after its formation in order to accept a wartime appointment to the United States Standards Board in Washington, D. C. Deeds later served as a member of the Aircraft Production Board, then as Acting Chief of the Equipment Division of the Signal Corps, for which he was commissioned a colonel in the regular Army. One of Deeds' greatest wartime contributions was directing the development of the Liberty engine, the only all American-produced airplane engine used in World I, which continued to power military and civilian airplanes for many years after the war ended. Several models of the Liberty engine are on display at the United States Air Force Museum.

Deeds' other aviation associations included helping to form the Pratt and Whitney Aircraft Company in 1925, serving as a director of Pan American Airways starting in 1931, purchasing the first private

and four feet eight inches high and weighed 530 pounds loaded, including 180 pounds of high explosives. It had a speed of 120 miles per hour and a range of 75 miles.

The *Bug*'s yellow poplar propeller was designed by Orville Wright, consulting engineer to Dayton Wright. The four-cylinder 40-horsepower engine was designed by Ralph DePalma, a noted race car driver, and C. H. Wills, a former Ford Motor Car Company engineer. Kettering developed the pre-set internal control system that guided the *Bug* to its target and then shut off its motor and released its wings,

Orville Wright's bedroom at the Wright mansion, *Hawthorn Hill*. Orville's bed, dresser and the picture on the wall are on display at the Kettering-Moraine Museum.

luxury airplane manufactured in the United States (an all-metal ten-passenger Ford Tri-Motor) in 1928 and installing the first plane on a private yacht (a five-passenger Sikorsky amphibian).

Deeds probably is best known for his partnership with Charles F. Kettering and for his career at the National Cash Register Company (NCR). Deeds' association with Kettering led to the formation of Dayton Engineering Laboratories Company (Delco) and other business enterprises which are described under SL 4. Deeds' career at NCR included 26 years as chief executive officer and chairman of the board before his retirement in 1957. Deeds died at *Moraine Farm* on July 1, 1960 at the age of 86.

Moraine Farm was named for the geological formations underlying the area, called terminal moraines, which were formed when the most recent glacier to cover the Miami Valley started to retreat about 40,000 years ago. The moraines consist of mounds of debris, such as rocks and stones, that became embedded in the ice and were pushed forward as the glacier moved south, then were left behind when the ice melted as the glacier retreated north.

The buildings at *Moraine Farm* were erected between 1912 and 1923. Among those still standing are the English manor-style residence and an observatory with a seven inch refractory telescope. At one time totaling 600 acres, today only a few acres surrounding the residence remain. A Huber Homes development now occupies 125 acres of what was once Deeds' private airport.

Moraine Farm is now owned by NCR Corporation, which maintains the property as a guesthouse and meeting place.

Moraine Farm is not open to the public.

SL 4   Kettering-Moraine Museum
35 Moraine Circle South
Kettering, Ohio 45439

The Kettering-Moraine Museum is a local history museum for two south of Dayton suburbs, Kettering and Moraine. The museum's displays include a Wright brothers exhibit and the original Deeds Barn. A replica of the barn is at Carillon Historical Park (SL 1).

The Wright brothers exhibit contains a large collection of furniture from *Hawthorn Hill* (SL 11), the Wright mansion, and many of the family's artifacts and personal belongings.

The restored Deeds Barn, which originally stood behind Edward A. Deeds' house at 319 Central Avenue in Dayton, was the home of the Barn Gang, a group of Dayton inventors. The gang originated with Deeds and Charles F. Kettering when the two formed a handshake partnership in 1908 to develop improvements to the automobile. Or as Deeds said to Kettering, "There is a river of gold running past us. Why can't we throw out a little dam and sluice some of it our way?" At the time, Deeds and Kettering were employed at the National Cash Register Company (NCR) and could work on the barn projects only in the evenings and on weekends.

Shortly after starting work on their initial project in a workshop set up in the loft of the barn, Deeds and Kettering were joined by several of their NCR associates. Among them were William A. Chryst, Kettering's assistant in the Inventions 3 Department at NCR, William Anderson, Zerbe Bradford, William Mooney, John Reece, Ralph Todd, A.I. Phillips, John Lipes, Albert Koffer, John Sheets, Robert Demaree and W, G. Johns. In 1909 Kettering quit his NCR job to devote full time to the barn projects.

Upon the successful development of their first product, an electric automobile ignition system to replace the magneto then in use, Deeds and Kettering formed The Dayton Engineering Laboratories Company (Delco) July 21, 1909 and set up an office in the United Brethren Building (CL 6)). In 1911, upon the completion of their second product, the automobile self-starter which eliminated the need for hand cranking, they branched out into manufacturing, renting space in the Beaver Power Building at 35 South St. Clair Street in Dayton.

After the success of the self-starter things moved rapidly. In 1914 Deeds quit his job at NCR to work full time at Delco. Two years later Deeds and Kettering sold Delco to The United Motors Corporation for $9,000,000 in cash and stock. When United Motors became a part of General Motors Corporation (GM) in 1918, Delco became a GM division. In 1920 Kettering joined GM as head of the newly-formed GM Research Corporation, serving as a GM vice president until his retirement in 1947.

At its present location, the two-story frame Deeds Barn contrasts sharply with the sprawling highly-mechanized GM complex located immediately to its rear. The "idea hatchery," as Kettering called it, in the loft of the barn was basically a machine shop with a long work bench, small tools, a milling machine, a drill press, an

The Deeds barn at its original location behind Edward A. Deeds' house at 319 Central Avenue in Dayton. Deeds and Charles F. Kettering started their partnership here in 1908. The original building is now an exhibit at the Kettering-Moraine museum.

engine lathe, a tool grinder, a forge, an oscillograph and one ten-horsepower motor.

Kettering was an early aviation enthusiast, taking his first airplane ride at the Wright Huffman Prairie flying school (EA 2) in 1912 in a Wright Model B piloted by Howard Rinehart. Rinehart later made several record-breaking cross-country flights with Kettering; then taught him to pilot an airplane himself after World War I. As a pilot Kettering became one of the first to fly by instruments -- at a time when most pilots considered instrument flying for "sissies."

As an inventor and engineer Kettering's contributions to aviation included development of the ignition system for the Liberty air-

The Dayton Wright Airplane Co, South Field - May 14-18.

Dayton Wright Airplane Company DeHaviland-4 in 1918. The DH-4 was the only all American-produced airplane to see action in World War I. From the original glass negative.

plane engine, work on improved aircraft fuels and development of the first guided missile, described under SL 3. Kettering's approach to engineering problems paralleled that of the Wright brothers who, he said, "flew right through the smoke screen of impossibility."

Charles F. Kettering (1876-1958) was inducted into the National Aviation Hall of Fame (see EA 1) in 1979.

Kettering's home, *Ridgeleigh Terrace*, which he occupied from 1914 until his death on November 25, 1958 at the age of 82, was built on a hill off Southern Boulevard in Kettering, next to Deeds' *Moraine Farm* (SL 3). It was destroyed in a fire in December 1994, but is being rebuilt by the present owner, the Kettering Medical Center. The Center includes the Kettering Memorial Hospital, located next to the home on land donated by Kettering's heirs. The city of Kettering is named for Charles F. Kettering. The Kettering-Moraine Museum owns a large collection of Kettering's papers, artifacts and memorabilia.

The Kettering-Moraine Museum, founded in 1972, is maintained by the Kettering-Moraine Museum and Historical Society. The one-story cement block main building was formerly the Kettering Court Building and before that served as the community center for a government World War II housing project.

The museum's exhibits include several restored historical buildings and a series of displays about the Watervliet Shaker Community, a religious settlement founded in 1806 on part of what was later the old State Farm off Patterson Road. The site is now part of the Miami Valley Research Park.

The museum is open 1:00 to 5:00 p.m. Sundays. Group tours are available at other times by telephoning the museum office at 937-299-2722. Admission is $1.00 for 12 and older; under 12 free.

SL 5   Former Dayton Wright Airplane Company
          Main Plant
        Power Train Group Moraine Engine Plant
        General Motors Corporation
        4100 Springboro Road
        Moraine, Ohio 45439

The main plant of the Dayton Wright Airplane Company was located on part of the site now occupied by the General Motors Power Train Group Moraine Engine Plant.

The Dayton Wright Airplane Company Mill Department at Plant 1 in 1918. From the original glass negative.

Dayton Wright was formed by Edward A. Deeds and Charles F. Kettering in April 1917 to manufacture airplanes for World War I and as a way of "keeping Dayton on the airplane map." Orville Wright also was associated with the company, serving as a member of the board and consulting engineer. Other board members included H.

E. Talbott, Sr. and his son H. E. Talbott, Jr., who later served as secretary of the Air Force under President Eisenhower.

Among the aircraft produced by Dayton Wright were two models listed in *Jane's 100 Significant Aircraft*: the DeHaviland-4, a World War I warplane, and the R. B. Racer, an advanced design civilian airplane.

The DeHaviland-4 (DH-4), the company's best-known model, was the only all American-produced airplane to see action in World War I. An American adaptation of a British airplane designed by Geoffrey de Haviland, the DH-4 was a two-seat open cockpit biplane equipped with a 420-horsepower Liberty 12 engine. It was 36 feet six inches long and ten feet four inches high, had a 42-foot six-inch wingspan and weighed 3,557 pounds. When fully armed the plane carried two .30-caliber Martin fixed machine guns, two .30-caliber Lewis flexible machine guns and 200 pounds of bombs suspended beneath the wings and fuselage. The price was $11,250.

Dayton Wright sub-contracted for many of the DH-4 parts, including the Liberty engine, which was made by five companies: Packard, Lincoln, Ford, General Motors and Nordyke and Marmon. Local suppliers included the National Cash Register Company (NCR), which manufactured the airspeed indicators and chronometric tachometers.

A total of 4,846 DH-4s were completed before Armistice was declared on November 11, 1918. Of these Dayton Wright built 3,106, with the remainder manufactured by the General Motors Fisher Body Division and the Standard Aircraft Corporation. Only 513 reached the front before the war ended and only 417 saw combat.

Although the DH-4 was designed as a warplane, its greatest usefulness came after the war when the large stock of brand new, no longer needed aircraft was modified for peacetime use as airmail planes, trainers, transports, ambulances, couriers and crop dusters. DH-4s also were used for experimental flights, including the first successful in-flight refueling, on June 27, 1922, over San Diego, California. The last DH-4 was retired in 1932. A restored DH-4 is on display at the United States Air Force Museum (EA 1).

The Dayton Wright R. B. Racer was designed specifically to

THE DAYTON WRIGHT AIRPLANE CO.
DAYTON, OHIO.
JUNE, 3-18.   PLANT-1.

The Dayton Wright Airplane Company Plant 1 while still under construction in June 1918. From the original glass negative.

compete in the 1920 Gordon Bennett race "to bring the Gordon Bennett Cup back to America." The Gordon Bennett Aviation Cup, for speed, was sponsored by James Gordon Bennett, Jr., publisher of the *New York Herald*. The 1920 race was the last of six. Unfortunately, the Dayton Wright airplane experienced a problem with its variable-camber gear, forcing it to drop out after the first turn of the race.

The R. B. Racer contrasted sharply with the open cockpit DH-4 built only two years earlier. The R. B. Racer was a single-seat monoplane with variable camber wings. It had a 21-foot two-inch wing span, was 22 feet eight inches long and eight feet high, weighed 1,400 pounds empty and had a maximum speed of 200 miles per hour. The streamlined balsa wood fuselage was covered with varnished veneer.

Advanced features included retractable landing wheels, an enclosed cabin with a large celluloid window on each side, and a sliding roof above the cockpit. The engine was a six-cylinder water-cooled 250-horsepower Hall-Scott Liberty Six. The single wooden propeller was manufactured by the Hartzell Walnut Propeller Company (NL 7). NCR made some of the instruments. Orville Wright acted as consulting engineer.

Other Dayton Wright airplanes included the Standard J-1, the XPS-1, the O.W.I. Aerial Sedan and the K.T.I. Cabin cruiser. The Standard J-1 was a World War I trainer. The XPS-1, an open cockpit fighter similar to the R. B. Racer, was the first United States Air Service airplane with a retractable landing gear. The O.W.I. Aerial Sedan and the K.T.I. Cabin Cruiser were closed cockpit civilian biplanes. The O.W.I. Aerial Sedan was the last Dayton Wright airplane on which Orville Wright worked.

Dayton Wright had two other plants in addition to its main plant (Plant 1) and the Experimental Station across the road at South Field (SL 3). Plant 2, located in a four-story brick building east of the railroad on Pearl Street in Miamisburg, manufactured over 20 parts, including control cables, landing gear and rear fuselages. The former Plant 2 building was demolished in the 1970s. Plant 3, located in two still-standing buildings at the General Motors Delphi Chassis Division Home Avenue Operations plant (WA 11), manufactured small parts, including metal fittings and steering wheels.

The first building occupied by Plant 1 was a one-story 270-by-1350-foot steel, concrete and brick structure, the largest of its kind in the state at that time. Originally constructed as a factory for The Domestic Engineering Company (formed to manufacture the rural electric system invented by Kettering), wartime priorities required it be turned over to Dayton Wright shortly before its completion. Subsequently the building was lengthened to 2,500 feet and additional buildings were added. The building was incorporated into the new General Motors Engine Plant during the 1980-1981 conversion. A door to the Dayton Wright safe discovered during the work is now on display at the Kettering-Moraine Museum (SL 4).

Plant 1 was located in the new community of Moraine, a city that grew out of the dream of real estate developer Adam Schantz, Jr. to create a model industrial town. Schantz's plan for the 882-acre tract south of Dayton called for 500 acres to be reserved for home sites, streets, a park, a school and a civic center, with the remainder to be developed as industrial sites and railroad yards. The city is named for the local geological formations called terminal moraines, the same origin as the name for *Moraine Farm* (SL 3).

In 1919, two years after its formation, the Dayton Wright Airplane Company was acquired by the General Motors Corporation (GM). Four years later, on June 1, 1923, GM ceased all airplane manufacture and experimentation when the company decided to concentrate on the automotive market.

After acquiring Dayton Wright in 1919, GM established two other enterprises in part of the unused factory space: the General Motors Research Corporation in 1920 and Frigidaire in 1921.

The GM Research Corporation was under the direction of Kettering, who had been associated with the company since GM's predecessor, The United Motors Corporation, bought Delco in 1916. Under the 1920 agreement, GM bought out all of Kettering's Dayton interests and Kettering became a full-time GM employee, serving as a vice president and member of the board. After the Research Corporation moved to Detroit in 1925 Kettering commuted between Detroit and his home in Dayton until his retirement in 1947.

Frigidaire grew out of the iceless ice box invented in 1915 by former Daytonian Alfred Mellowes and Rueben E. Bechtold of Ft. Wayne, Indiana. Originally called the Guardian Frigerator Company, the name was changed to Frigidaire after the company was acquired by GM in 1919. Through the years Frigidaire expanded into the manufacture of other household appliances and other products.

Delco Air Conditioning was spun off from Frigidaire as a separate unit in 1974. Then in 1979 General Motors sold Frigidaire to White Consolidated Industries of Cleveland, Ohio and the former Frigidaire facility was converted into two new plants: an engine plant, which produces diesel engines, and an assembly plant, which produces trucks.

A plaque commemorating the Dayton Wright Airplane Company factory was presented to the Moraine Engine Plant by Aviation Trail, Inc. at a community dinner on September 15, 1983 in celebration of General Motors' 75th anniversary. The plaque is installed on a pedestal in the landscaped entrance to the plant office.

The Power Train Group Moraine Engine Plant is not open to the public.

SL 6   Wright Seaplane Base
Great Miami River at Sellers Road Bridge
Moraine, Ohio 45439

The Great Miami River from a short distance south of the Sellers Road bridge north to the Dayton Power and Light Company's former Frank M. Tait Station served as the Wright seaplane base where Orville Wright tested Wright Company seaplanes from 1911 to 1913. Models tested included modified Model Bs, the Model CH hydroplane and the Model G aeroboat.

Although Wilbur and Orville Wright first experimented with a water-based plane in 1907, the brothers' first successful model was the B-1 hydroplane, built in 1911. The B-1, the first Wright machine purchased by the United States Navy, was a pontoon-equipped adaptation of the popular Model B land-based airplane described under WA 10. A second plane of the same type, the B-2, was purchased by the Navy a year later. And the first civilian version was announced in the 1912 Wright Company catalogue with the notation that the Wright brothers experimented with hydroplanes "as far back as 1907."

The Model CH hydroplane, an adaptation of the Model C land-based airplane described under WA 11, was first announced July 1, 1913. Two versions, one with a pair of pontoons attached to the skids and a later version with a single pontoon, were tested by Orville in over 100 flights from May to July 1913.

The Model G Aeroboat, first announced September 10, 1913, was more than an adaptation of a Wright land-based airplane. It was a totally new machine designed for takeoff and landing on water only. The Aeroboat, a biplane, had two pusher propellers and a short hull fuselage resembling a boat. It was powered by a Wright Six-Sixty engine, the last engine model produced by The Wright Company. A flag mounted on the front of the machine served as a primitive flight instrument, indicating whether the airplane was flying straight ahead or was in a bank, climb or dive. Model Gs were purchased by both the Navy and civilians.

A partially reconstructed Model G is on display at the Neil Armstrong Air and Space Museum in Wapakoneta, Ohio, 60 miles north of Dayton.

The Model G Aeroboat was designed by Grover Loening, a Wright Company aeronautical engineer and factory manager from July 1913 to July 1914. The first in the United States to receive a graduate degree in aeronautical science (from Columbia University), Loening later formed his own company, the Loening Aeronautical Engineering Corporation, in New York City, and gained fame as an aircraft designer and manufacturer.

Loening aircraft included the Amphibian (1924 to 1930), a single propeller tractor biplane with a retractable landing gear that enabled it to land on either land or water. The plane was powered by an inverted Liberty engine, an innovation developed by the Power Plant Branch at McCook Field (NL 1) in 1923 to eliminate a blind spot in front that interfered with visibility.

Loening Amphibians were used as military airplanes, company airplanes and airliners as well as for explorations and surveys. Landmark flights included the 1925 Byrd-MacMillan Arctic Expedition, the 1926-1927 United States Army Pan-American Goodwill Tour of 25 Central and South American countries and the 1926 and 1927 United States Navy Alaskan surveys. The *San Francisco*, one of the five Loening Amphibians to make the 1926-1927 goodwill tour, is on display at the United States Air Force Museum (EA 1).

Grover Loening (1888-1976) was inducted into the National Aviation Hall of Fame (see EA 1) in 1969.

The Wright brothers first attempted to construct a water-based airplane in 1907 when they attached an airplane engine and propellers to a two-hulled boat to form a hydrofoil, which they tested on the Great Miami River near the Main Street bridge on March 20-21. Unfortunately, a flood on the night of March 21 cut short the tests, forcing the brothers to drop the project. The Wrights had hoped to interest the Navy in their invention by demonstrating the hydrofoil at the Naval Review on April 26, 1907 at Hampton Roads, Virginia. The engine that powered their 1907 hydrofoil is on display at The Engineers Club (CL 4).

The popularity of seaplanes in the post-World War I era grew

Orville Wright with a Wright hydroplane on the Great Miami River in 1913.

out of a scarcity of airfields necessary for the safe landing of land-based machines. Seaplanes, on the other hand, "carried their airfields on their bottoms" for most urban areas were located on or near a body of water. The modern term "airport," first used by then Secretary of Commerce Herbert Hoover in 1925, originated with this concept of harbors, or ports, for airplanes.

The section of the Great Miami River where Orville Wright tested Wright Company hydroplanes had three advantages: freedom from man-made obstacles such as overhead wires and bridges, a bend in the river that enabled the aviator to take off north-south or east-west, depending on the prevailing wind, and a deep pool of water formed by a hydraulic dam south of the present Sellers Road Bridge.

The original dam, breached a number of years ago, was replaced in the late 1980s by a new dam a short distance upstream. The construction of the new dam made possible the establishment of a modern seaplane facility equipped with a concrete ramp and tie-downs on the shore that provide the seaplanes a safe anchorage in the variable levels of the river. The new seaplane base is now awaiting certification by the State and then by the Federal Aviation Administration.

The new seaplane base is next to the Moraine Airpark on the west bank of the river. On the other side of the river, near the new dam, are a boat ramp and parking areas, which can be reached through an entrance on Alex Road (where it meets Hydraulic Road) in West Carrollton. The area is one of a number of developed recreation areas located in the River Corridor that runs along the Great Miami River.

Another attraction along the river, on the west bank to the north of the Sellers Road Bridge, is the site of an ancient village occupied by the Fort Ancient Indians in the 12th century. The Dayton Museum of Natural History has erected a reconstruction of the village, which can be reached off West River Road. The site is listed on the National Register of Historic Places.

The Seaplane Base is near the southern end of the 28-mile River Corridor Bikeway, which runs along the Great Miami River from the Montgomery County-Warren County line north to Sinclair Park in Harrison Township.

SL 7   Pinnacle Hill
Pinnacle Road west of Vance Road
Moraine, Ohio 45418

Wilbur and Orville Wright's observations of the flight of birds at Pinnacle Hill led to the first breakthrough in their search for the secrets of powered flight, their wing-warping theory for lateral control.

The Wright brothers knew that an airplane, as an airborne vehicle, must be controlled on three axes: the level or horizontal (turning to the left or right), the vertical (climbing or descending) and the lateral (banking to the side or rolling back to the level). Others before the Wrights had developed techniques for level and vertical control, but none had solved the problem of lateral control. That was the Wright brothers' unique contribution to aircraft stability, their wing-warping technique for lateral control.

Techniques for turning right or left on a level plane (yaw) were proposed in the 18th century when early balloonists suggested using an adaptation of a ship's rudder to steer their aircraft. Techniques for climbing or descending (pitch) soon followed when the concept of the rudder was modified into a horizontal, rather than upright, rudder or elevator. Sir George Caylay used a single implement, a cruciform tail, a combined rudder and elevator, to control yaw and pitch on his classic 1804 model of a glider. However, no previous technology suggested a solution for lateral control; that is, rotation around a line through the center of the plane's fuselage, or roll. Many earlier experimenters even refused to recognize a need for lateral control, reasoning that active pilot control was not necessary because lateral stability could be built into the machine.

The Wright's experience with bicycles; that is, the difficulty of maintaining equilibrium, or balance, on a two-wheeled vehicle, convinced them that active pilot control of roll (lateral control) was just as important as the control of yaw or pitch. And their observations of the flight of birds at Pinnacle Hill from 1897 to 1899 showed them the way.

Wilbur Wright standing to the right of a pinnacle in 1898. The pinnacles were unique geological formations on the hill where the Wright brothers observed the flight of birds from 1897 to 1899.

The Wrights developed their wing-warping theory in the summer of 1899 after observing the buzzards at Pinnacle Hill twisting the tips of their wings as they soared into the wind so that the angle of attack of one wing was greater than that of the other. The brothers theorized that roll could be controlled by applying the birds' wing-warping technique to the wings of an airplane. Wilbur discovered how to implement the theory a short time later as he idly twisted an empty bicycle innertube box while waiting on a customer in the brothers' bicycle shop. As he toyed with the box, Wilbur found that by twisting the forward corner of one end and the rear corner of the other end, the top and bottom of the box would each present a different angle.

The Wrights successfully tested their wing-warping theory on a biplane kite in September 1899 during flights in a field off West Third Street. The kite, five feet from wing to wing and 13 inches from front to back, was controlled by four cords, one attached to each end of the two wings with the other ends fastened to two sticks held by the operator. The operator maintained front to rear balance (pitch) by inclining the sticks in the same direction and lateral balance (roll) by inclining the sticks in opposite directions (the wing-warping technique). The brothers perfected their control system during a series of tests with man-carrying gliders of their design at Kitty Hawk, North Carolina in 1900, 1901 and 1902.

The Wrights' 1900 glider, flown at Kitty Hawk in October, was a biplane with a 165-square foot wing area, an ash and white pine airframe and bias-cut French sateen covering. It weighed 190 pounds, including the operator, and had a speed of 20 to 30 miles per hour. The elevator was placed at the front (a configuration called "the canard" because of its supposed resemblance to a duck), a position the Wrights thought would help prevent dives. The brothers flew the glider sometimes as a kite and sometimes manned, with the operator lying prone on the lower wing to lessen wind resistance. Left behind at Kitty Hawk when the Wrights returned to Dayton, the glider was wrecked in a storm in 1901.

The 1901 glider was a larger version of the 1900 model and was the largest glider ever flown up to that time. As in the earlier model, it had only two controls, the elevator and the wing-warping mechanism. The Wrights made between 50 to 100 glides at Kitty Hawk in July and August, covering distances ranging from 20 feet to almost 100 feet. This glider, also left behind when the Wrights returned to Dayton, was destroyed upon their return the next year to make room for their 1902 model.

The 1902 glider was the first to have three-axes control: a moveable elevator in front to control pitch, the wing-warping mechanism to control roll and a new fixed vertical double rudder to control yaw. The rudder later was changed to a moveable single fin connected to the wing-warping mechanism so the pilot could operate both controls at the same time by shifting his body in the hip cradle as he lay prone on the lower wing. Not until the 1905 Flyer were the rudder and wing-warping controls separated, providing independent control of each of the three axes for the first time.

The 1902 glider was 16 feet long, weighed 112 pounds, and had a wing area of 305 square feet. From September 19 to October 24, the Wrights made between 700 and 1,000 glides with their third glider, the longest covering 662.5 feet. At the end of these tests, Wilbur and Orville knew they had a controllable man-carrying machine needing only the addition of a motor and propellers to achieve powered flight.

The 1902 glider was destroyed in 1903 when it became dilapidated and unsafe after the Wrights made between 60 and 100 glides as a prelude to testing their new powered machine, the 1903 Flyer I, first successfully flown on December 17. The Flyer I, as well as the Flyer II and Flyer III, are described under SL 1.

In the Wrights' day Pinnacle Hill, or the Pinnacles, was a popular picnic spot west of the Great Miami River to the south of Dayton, easily accessible by bicycle from the brothers' West Side Dayton home. At that time the Pinnacles was dotted with about 20 equipped shelterhouses that could be rented for a day's outing in the picturesque natural setting. Ranging from 60 to 80 feet high, the pinnacles created updrafts that attracted buzzards and other birds, thus providing an ideal observation point for the Wrights to study the mechanism of flight as the birds soared in the strong winds.

Pinnacle Hill is one of a number of ridges in the Miami Valley that were created after the last glacier to cover the area, the Wisconsin Continental Drift, retreated north about 40,000 years ago. The ridges, long, narrow land elevations, are formed of till, a combination of clay, gravel and broken rocks that were carried down from Canada in the ice as the glacier pushed its way south to form the Miami Lobe, which extended from Xenia, Ohio to Connersville, Indiana and as far south as the northern edge of Cincinnati, Ohio. The melting ice from the glacier created the present-day river system. The ridges were formed from the harder materials that remained after the softer materials carried down by the glacier eroded. The moraines for which *Moraine Farm* (SL 3) and the city of Moraine are named were created by the same glacier.

The pinnacles were located on a bluff on the west bank of the Great Miami River overlooking the section of the river where Orville Wright tested Wright Company hydroplanes at the Wright Seaplane Base (SL 6). The former Dayton Wright Airplane Company factory (SL 5) is located across the river on the east bank and *Moraine Farm* on a hill above it.

Today a farm across the street from the Hickory Creek Nursing Center marks the location of the pinnacles area. The property has been unoccupied since the death of its last owner, Gourley Darroch, who once was a visitor at Orville Wright's summer home on Lambert Island in Canada. The pinnacles themselves were destroyed in a Pinnacle Road construction project.

SL 8   Wright B Flyer Hangar
               Dayton-Wright Brothers Airport
               10550 Springboro Pike
               Miamisburg, Ohio 45342

The Wright B Flyer is a flyable look-alike of the world's first production model airplane, the Wright Model B manufactured by The Wright Company in Dayton (see WA 10 and WA 11). It is housed in a hangar similar to the Wrights' 1910 hangar at their Huffman Prairie flying field (EA 3).

Built in 1910-1911, the Model B was a two-seat dual-control biplane. It was used extensively to train new pilots at the Wright flying school at Huffman Prairie and elsewhere, was among the first airplanes purchased by the United States Navy and Army and figured in a number of historic flights, including the first commercial flight, in 1910 (see WA 10).

A single-seat modified version of the Model B, called the EX and piloted by Calbraith "Cal" Perry Rodgers, made the first flight across the United States, in 1911. Rodgers learned to fly in a Model B at the Wrights' Huffman Prairie flying school in June 1911. At the end of his training he purchased a Model B, in which he gave exhibition flights for several months before embarking on his historic flight.

Rodgers' flight was made in response to an offer of a $50,000 prize from newspaper publisher William Randolph Hearst to the first to fly across the United States from one ocean to the other in 30 days during a specified time period -- October 1, 1910 to October 1, 1911.

Rodgers' airplane was named the *Vin Fiz* after a grape-flavored soft drink being promoted by his sponsor, the Armour Meat Packing Company of Chicago. The support system provided by the sponsor included a three-car private train with a "hangar" car and passenger sleeping and eating accommodations. Accompanying him as lead mechanic was Charley Taylor (see WA 7), who had taken a leave of absence from his job as airplane mechanic for the Wright brothers. Takeoff was from Sheepshead Bay, New York on September 17.

Contest rules stipulated that the entire flight must be made in the same airplane, although there was no restriction on the number or type of repairs that could be made. By the time Rodgers completed his journey no more than two or three small parts remained of the original machine.

Wright Model B Flyer look-alike at the Dayton Airshow in 1985

In the end, Rodgers took about three months to complete his cross-country trip, landing at Long Beach, California on December 10, after a series of short hops with about 80 stops and just over 82 hours actual flight time. The most serious delay came at the very end when the crash of his airplane on November 12 near Pasadena, California left him with numerous injuries, including broken bones, burns and lacerations. About a month later, while still on crutches, he flew the few remaining miles to Long Beach, triumphantly landing with his wheels resting in the Pacific ocean. Tragically, Rodgers died less than four months later of injuries received in a crash of his airplane at Long Beach on April 8, 1912.

Although Rodgers failed to win the prize because he exceeded the time limit, he did complete the journey, earning him the honor of being the first to fly across the country. Twelve years later, in 1923, McCook Field (NL 1) test pilots Lieutenants Oakley G. Kelly and John A. Macready flew nonstop from New York to California in a little under 27 hours (see CL 7).

Calbraith P. Rodgers (1879-1912) was inducted into the National Aviation Hall of Fame (see EA 1) in 1964.

The Wright B Flyer look-alike was constructed by a group of volunteer aviation enthusiasts. It is owned and operated by the nonprofit Wright B Flyer, Inc. A modified original Model B is on display at the United States Air Force Museum (EA 1).

The project to construct a flyable replica of the Wright Model B was first suggested in 1974 as a way to celebrate the nation's bicentennial in 1976. However, various obstacles and delays prolonged the construction and Federal Aviation Administration (FAA) certification process well past the original target date. Finally, the look-alike (modified to meet FAA flight standards), "got off the ground" in 1982. Since then it has appeared at numerous aviation events around the world.

In addition to the Wright Model B look-alike, the hangar houses a one-half scale model of the Model B (for events such as parades) and the restored 1916 Ford Model T "staff car."

The airport on which the Model B Hangar is located was formerly called Dayton General Airport South. On December 18, 1995 it was formally renamed Dayton-Wright Brothers Airport in honor of Wilbur and Orville Wright. The airport is owned and operated by the City of Dayton.

The Wright B Flyer Hangar is open 9:00 a.m. to 2:30 p.m. Tuesday, Thursday and Saturday, except holidays. Admission is free. Orientation flights are available; call 937-885-2327 for information.

SL 9   International Women's Air and Space Museum
Asahel Wright House
26 North Main Street
Centerville, Ohio 45459

International Women's Air and Space Museum, Inc. operates a museum in the historic Asahel Wright House, one-time home of Wilbur and Orville Wright's great-uncle. The museum honors the contributions of women to aviation, from the pioneer pilots of the early 1900s to the current space age.

The museum's exhibits include a special display about Katharine Wright, Wilbur and Orville's sister, who encouraged and supported her brothers in their efforts to invent the airplane. It also contains an original flight suit worn by well-known aviatrix Amelia Earhart as well as numerous artifacts associated with other pioneer women aviators, including those who served in the military, from World War II to the present women astronauts.

International Women's Air and Space Museum, Inc. was established as a nonprofit corporation in 1976 as an offshoot of the Ninety-Nines, an international organization of women pilots. In 1986 the group moved its museum to the Asahel Wright House from temporary quarters at Scott Equipment Company on Leo Street in Dayton.

Currently, plans are under development for the construction of a large permanent museum in Dayton, on the south side of West Third Street at the west end of the West Third Street Bridge. The new museum will be part of a large redevelopment project to bring back the mostly-residential neighborhood called Wright-Dunbar Village, named in honor of its one-time residents Wilbur and Orville Wright and Paul Laurence Dunbar (see WA 9).

The renovated Asahel Wright house was once the home of Wilbur and Orville Wright's great-uncle, Asahel Wright, the brother of Dan Wright, Jr., their paternal grandfather. Asahel and Dan, Jr. moved from Connecticut to Centerville with their parents, Dan, Sr. and Sarah Freeman Wright. They arrived at the village on February 12, 1814 when Asahel was 28 years old and Dan, Jr., 23.

Asahel Wright operated a store in Centerville from 1816 to 1826 where he sold liquor, tobacco, tools and various dry goods. Previous to that he had a distillery near the present-day intersection of Far Hills Avenue and Alexandersville-Bellbrook Road. Distilleries were a popular local enterprise at that time because farmers found it much more profitable to turn their grain into liquor than to pay the extremely high cost of transporting it in its natural form to the distant eastern markets.

In 1820 Asahel married Martha Sweeny, who bore him seven children: Edmond Freeman, Samuel, Sara, John Quincy, Warren, Harriet and William. Six years after Asahel and Martha were married the family moved to a farm in Miami County, trading their Centerville farm plus $500 for the new property. The new farm was located in Bethel Township (in what is now the town of Phoneton) on the east side of present-day State Route 202. The property included a building that had once been a tavern, in which Asahel established the Wright Store. The National Road, now Route 40, later was constructed across the north end of the Wright farm. Asahel Wright died October 23, 1842 at the age of 56. He and other members of his family are buried in the cemetery of the Bethel Church, which adjoins the former Wright farm to the south.

Dan Wright, Jr. married Catherine Reeder in 1818. Three years later the family moved from Centerville to a farm in the "wilderness" of Rush County, Indiana, where Milton, father of Wilbur

The former home of Wilbur and Orville Wright's great-uncle, Asahel Wright, in Centerville. The restored house was dedicated in 1983.

and Orville, was born on November 17, 1828. In addition to Milton, Dan, Jr. and Catherine were the parents of Samuel, Harvey, George (who died in infancy), Sarah and William. After moving to Indiana, Dan, Jr. "got religion" and even refused to sell his corn to a distiller. His religious convictions were instilled in his children, with all his sons who reached adulthood entering the ministry. And his distaste for liquor carried over to his grandsons Wilbur and Orville, neither of whom drank liquor or smoked tobacco. Dan Wright, Jr. died in 1861 at the age of 70.

Wilbur and Orville's Ohio roots go back to their great-great-grandparents, John and Catharine Benham Van Cleve, the grandparents of Dan, Jr.'s wife, Catherine Reeder. John Van Cleve and

Catharine Benham were married in New Jersey in 1771 and became the parents of six children: Benjamin, Anna, Margaret, William, Mary and Amey. The family moved from New Jersey to Cincinnati, Ohio in 1790 and the following year John was killed and scalped by Indians while working in an out lot on his farm. In 1796 Margaret married George Reeder of Centerville; then in 1818 their daughter, Catherine, married Dan Wright, Jr.

About two years after John Van Cleve's death, his widow married Samuel Thompson and bore him four children. On April 1, 1796 Catharine Van Cleve Thompson became the first white woman to set foot in Dayton when she, her second husband, their children Sarah and Matthew Thompson, and her children Benjamin and Mary Van Cleve, arrived with the first boatload of settlers after an 11-day trip up the Great Miami River from Cincinnati. Samuel Thompson drowned in the Great Miami River in 1815. Catharine Van Cleve Thompson, for whom the Wright brothers named their Van Cleve bicycle, died in 1837.

Wilbur and Orville Wright also were direct descendants of a 16th century English nobleman, Sir John Wright. A descendant of Sir John's, Deacon Samuel Wright, migrated to Massachusetts sometime before 1638, the first of their ancestors to settle in America.

In the fall of 1892, the year the Wright brothers bought their first bicycles and decided to open their first bicycle shop (WA 8), Wilbur and Orville made an unintended bicycle trip to Centerville, which Wilbur described in a letter to their sister Katharine, dated September 18, 1892. He wrote that after leaving home at 4:45 p.m. for a late-afternoon ride to Miamisburg via the Cincinnati Pike (present-day Patterson Boulevard-Dixie Highway), they decided to stop at the Fairgrounds to run around the racetrack a few times. Apparently disoriented after circling the track, the brothers resumed their journey on the Lebanon Pike (present-day Main Street-Far Hills Avenue) to the east of the Fairgrounds instead of the Cincinnati Pike on the west. Wilbur told about climbing the "classic heights of Runnymede" and the succeeding "wobbles" of the road, each higher than the one before, until they at last came upon a farmer mowing hay, who informed them they were headed towards Centerville, "the highest point in the county," rather than Miamisburg, seven miles to the west. Wilbur concluded, "I had for some time had a curiosity to see the place where grandfather Wright first settled when he came West but I had not expected to come upon it so unceremoniously."

Asahel Wright purchased the Centerville house from Aaron Nutt, a Centerville founder, for $150 on August 16, 1816. The original one-story stone structure, erected about 1806, was later enlarged by adding a second story and then by building a two-story frame addition in 1860. The small one-story frame building at the front of the lot, constructed about 1830, probably was used as a store.

The Asahel Wright house was renovated through a community effort involving public grants and volunteers. The building was dedicated July 4, 1983 during a ceremony attended by Ivonette Wright Miller and Horace Wright, the children of Wilbur and Orville's brother Lorin. The house is now owned by the city of Centerville.

The Asahel Wright house is one of 14 early (1803-1840) stone houses still standing in Centerville, the largest concentration of such houses in the state. The houses are constructed of local limestone known as "Dayton marble," the same type of stone that was used in building the locks of the Miami and Erie Canal.

One of the early stone houses, the Walton House at 89 West Franklin Street, contains a museum maintained by the Centerville Historical Society. The house is named for its previous owners, William and Miriam (Mary) Walton, who bequeathed the property to the Historical Society. William Walton was the brother of Edith Deeds, wife of Colonel Edward A. Deeds, owner of *Moraine Farm* (SL 3). The Historical Society owns a collection of letters from Edith Deeds to the Waltons.

The International Women's Air and Space Museum is open from 10:00 a.m. to 4:00 p.m. Thursday, Friday and Saturday. Admission is free.

SL 10 Wright Memorial Library
1776 Far Hills Avenue
Oakwood, Ohio 45419

The Wright Memorial Library, the public library for the city of Oakwood, is named in honor of Wilbur, Orville and Katharine Wright.

Orville was a member of the library board from 1934 to 1946, serving as vice president for 11 of the 12 years. Known for his reluctance to speak in public, Orville is said to have accepted the office only on condition that he never be asked to chair a meeting, and the condition stuck. The one time the president was absent, the story goes, Orville was adamant in his refusal to chair the meeting, so the meeting was cancelled and everyone went home.

The Oakwood Library dates back to some time before 1913 when the Library Committee of the Oakwood Efficiency League established a library at Briar Hill, home of committee member Sarah Parrott. The Oakwood Board of Education took over operation of the Library in 1917, housing it first at Harmon School and later in its own building at 45 Park Avenue (now The Little Exchange), which was donated to the Library by board member John F. Fletcher.

The current library building was named in honor of Wilbur, Orville and Katharine Wright upon its opening in 1939. Expanded three times since, the latest addition, opened in 1983, features two stained glass windows, one depicting the first flight and the other the future of flight.

Library hours are 9:00 a.m. to 9:00 p.m. Monday through Friday, 9:00 a.m. to 5:00 p.m. Saturday and 1:00 to 5:00 p.m. Sunday.

Hawthorn Hill, the Wright mansion in Oakwood, in 1915.

SL 11 *Hawthorn Hill*
901 Harman Avenue
Oakwood, Ohio 45419

Hawthorn Hill was the home of Orville Wright, his father, Bishop Milton Wright, and his sister Katharine. The Bishop lived there until his death in 1917, Katharine until her marriage in 1926 and Orville until his death in 1948. Although he helped plan the house, Wilbur never lived there, dying of typhoid fever in 1912, two years before *Hawthorn Hill* was completed in the spring of 1914.

Hawthorn Hill was named for the many hawthorn trees growing on its steeply-sloping 17-acre site in the Dayton suburb of Oakwood. Purchased by Wilbur and Orville in 1910, the wooded hill provided an ideal setting for the southern-style mansion, a style the brothers first admired when they demonstrated their airplane for the United States Army at Fort Myer, Virginia in 1908 and 1909.

Two large pillared verandas dominate the exterior of the Wright mansion, one in the rear overlooking the city of Dayton and one in front facing the circular driveway. Of particular interest inside are a unique circular shower that Orville designed for his bathroom and a niche in a wall of the foyer built especially to display the bronze sculpture presented to Wilbur and Orville by the Aero Club of Sarthe, France during their 1909 trip to Europe.

The mansion's furnishings were conservative, yet elegant; for example, beige carpeting in the living room, made to order in Donegal, Ireland, complemented the gold damask wallcovering. The furniture, made by Berkey and Gay, known as the "sterling" of the furniture world, was selected by Orville and Katharine during a four-day trip to the factory in Grand Rapids, Michigan. Much of the furniture is on display at the Kettering-Moraine Museum (SL 4).

Carrie Kayler Grumbach, an employee of the Wright family for almost 50 years, was in charge of housekeeping at *Hawthorn Hill*. Carrie first came to work for the family in 1900 when she was hired to help with the housework at 7 Hawthorn Street (WA 4) and stayed until Orville's death in 1948.

Hawthorn Hill was the scene of two weddings and two funerals. The weddings were those of lvonette and Leontine Wright, daughters of Wilbur and Orville's brother Lorin. lvonette married Harold Miller in June 1919 and Leontine married John Jameson in June 1923. Harold Miller later served as co-executor of Orville's estate. The funerals were for Milton and Katharine.

Bishop Milton Wright died in his sleep on April 3, 1917 at the age of 88. The funeral was held on April 5, with burial in Woodland Cemetery (SL 12). Milton's career as a minister, teacher, editor and publisher spanned 50 years, from 1855, when he began a four-year stint as an itinerant minister, until his retirement in 1905 after serving

Katharine Wright at her graduation from Oberlin College in 1898.

Henry Haskell, husband of Katharine Wright. Henry and Katharine were married in 1926.

24 years as a bishop in the Church of the United Brethren in Christ. He was instrumental in establishing the United Theological Seminary in Dayton when he introduced the enabling legislation at the Church's 1869 Annual Conference. In 1859 Milton married Susan Catherine Koerner in Hartsville, Indiana, where the two had met while Susan was a student at the local college. Milton and Susan became the parents of twins who died in infancy and five children who lived to adulthood: Wilbur and Orville; two older sons, Reuchlin and Lorin; and a daughter, Katharine.

Katharine Wright Haskell died of pneumonia in Kansas City, Missouri on March 3, 1929 at the age of 54, less than three years after marrying widower Henry Haskell, an editor of the *Kansas City Star*, on November 20,1926. Katharine and Henry had known each other since they were students at Oberlin College, Oberlin, Ohio, and Katharine was a friend of Henry's first wife. Katharine's funeral was held on March 6, 1929. Her grave now lies between the graves of her brothers Wilbur and Orville in Woodland Cemetery.

An 1898 graduate of Oberlin College, Katharine was a history, English and Latin teacher, first at Dayton's Steele High School until 1908 and later (for a short time during World War I) at the private Moraine Park School. Moraine Park was located in Charles F. Kettering's renovated greenhouse on Southern Boulevard from 1917 to 1927. Among the school's board members were Kettering (see SL 4), Edward A. Deeds (see SL 3) and Orville Wright.

Katharine is often credited with starting the hobble skirt fashion during a 1909 trip to Europe with Wilbur and Orville when, as a passenger in their airplane, she tied a rope around the bottom of her skirt to keep it from flying up. However, Mrs. Hart O. Berg, wife of the Wrights' European agent, was the first to tie her skirt in this manner when she became the first woman to fly in an airplane, on October 7, 1908, in a machine piloted by Wilbur at Le Mans, France.

The two older Wright brothers had established their own households before the move to *Hawthorn Hill*. Reuchlin married Lulu Billheimer in 1886 and had four children: Catherine, Helen, Herbert and Bertha. The family moved to Kansas City about 1890 where Reuchlin worked as a bookkeeper for a short time before taking up

Orville Wright, left, and Charles Lindbergh in the rear seat of a government car at Wright Field in 1927, shortly after Lindbergh became the first to fly nonstop across the Altantic.

farming. He died in 1920 at the age of 59 and is buried in Kansas City.

Lorin married lvonette Stokes in 1892 and also had four children: Milton, lvonette, Leontine and Horace. Lorin remained in Dayton, where he became president of the Miami Wood Specialty Company and served as a member of the Dayton City Commission in the 1920s. Miami Wood manufactured wooden toys, including model airplanes with an advertiser's name that were used for promotions. Some of the firm's machinery was designed by Orville, who also developed one of its earliest products, a toy called Flips and Flops that involved two clowns and a trapeze. Lorin died in 1939 at the age of 77. He and his wife, Ivonette, are buried in Woodland Cemetery.

Hawthorn Hill represented material success to Orville Wright. Here he enjoyed a comfortable lifestyle, conducting research at his North Broadway laboratory (WA 6); taking part in community activities; continuing his father's genealogical research; driving around in his automobile, first an air-cooled Franklin, then an Essex Terraplane presented to him by the Hudson Motor Car Company; entertaining distinguished visitors and summering at Lambert Island, his 26-acre private island in Georgian Bay, Ontario, Canada.

Among Orville's guests at *Hawthorn Hill* were aviation pioneer Glenn L. Martin, inventors Alexander Graham Bell and Thomas A. Edison, industrialists Henry and Edsel Ford, and Charles A. Lindbergh, the first to fly nonstop across the Atlantic, on May 20, 1927. Lindbergh's visit a few weeks after his famous flight drew a huge crowd to the lawn of *Hawthorn Hill* once word of his presence leaked out. Shouting for a glimpse of the hero, the unruly mob trampled the grass and shrubbery and was dispersed only after Lindbergh agreed to appear briefly on the second floor balcony.

Hawthorn Hill is now owned by NCR Corporation, which purchased the house and remaining acreage shortly after Orville's death. (Part of the original 17 acres had been sold earlier). NCR completely redecorated the mansion for use as a company guesthouse, except for Orville's library, which remains exactly as it was the day he died, even to the book he was reading about his friend Colonel Edward A. Deeds, which still rests on the special reading stand he had built. And four pieces of the original Berkey and Gay furniture remain in the dining room: two sideboards, a table and a buffet containing two secret silver drawers.

Hawthorn Hill is listed on the National Register of Historic Places and is a National Historic Landmark.

Hawthorn Hill is not open to the public.

SL 12   Woodland Cemetery
118 Woodland Avenue
Dayton, Ohio 45409

Wilbur and Orville Wright and members of their family, as well as some of the others associated with sites on Dayton's Aviation Trail, are buried in Woodland Cemetery.

Wilbur (1867-1912) and Orville (1871-1948) Wright are buried in the Wright family plot, together with their father, Bishop Milton Wright (1828-1917), their mother, Susan Koerner Wright (1831-1889), and their sister, Katharine Wright Haskell (1874-1929).

Lorin Wright (1862-1939) and his wife Ivonette Stokes Wright (1865-1940) are buried overlooking the lake, several rows uphill from the southeast corner of the lake.

Charles Franklin Kettering (1876-1958), a founder of the Dayton Wright Airplane Company (SL 5), is interred in the Woodland Mausoleum, together with his son, Eugene Williams Kettering (1908-1969), leader of the campaign to establish the current United States Air Force Museum (EA 1).

Colonel Edward A. Deeds (1874-1960), owner of *Moraine Farm* (SL 3), is interred in the Deeds family mausoleum.

James Middleton Cox (1870-1957), Dayton newspaper publisher and former Governor of Ohio, for whom the James M. Cox Dayton International Airport (NL 11) is named, is buried in front of the Deeds mausoleum.

George W Hartzell (1869-1933) and his son, Robert Norris Hartzell (1896-1968), of the Hartzell Walnut Propeller Company (NL 7), are buried across the road from the Deeds mausoleum, a short distance to the south.

Lieutenant Frank Stuart Patterson (1896-1918), for whom Patterson Field (see EA 4) was named, is buried on the Patterson Knoll, together with other members of the prominent Patterson family, including John Henry Patterson (1844-1922), founder of the National Cash Register Company and donor of Hills and Dales Park (SL 2).

Paul Laurence Dunbar (1872-1906), internationally famous black poet who was associated with Wilbur and Orville Wright in their printing business (WA 2), is buried a short distance northeast of the Wright family plot.

Catharine Van Cleve Thompson (1756-1837), great-great-grandmother of Wilbur and Orville Wright, is buried in the Van Cleve family plot along with her grandson, John W. Van Cleve (1801-1858), leader of the group that founded Woodland Cemetery. (Catharine's remains were moved from an earlier cemetery after Woodland was opened.)

Woodland Cemetery was established in 1842 by the nonprofit Woodland Cemetery Association on a 40-acre hillside in what was then a suburb of Dayton. The sale of some of the trees on the heavily wooded property, purchased for $60 an acre, helped finance the initial operation and provide an endowment for perpetual care.

Now expanded to almost 200 acres, Woodland Cemetery also serves as an arboretum, with more than 3,000 trees, including over 80 identified species. A lookout toward the Wyoming Street side of the cemetery provides a panoramic view of the city of Dayton.

The Romanesque gateway, chapel and office at the Woodland Avenue entrance, completed in 1889, are listed on the National Register of Historic Places. A unique feature of the chapel is its large Tiffany window, called one of the finest Tiffany windows in the country.

A map of the cemetery can be obtained from the cemetery office, located immediately inside the Woodland Avenue gate.

The University of Dayton (UD), the largest independent university in Ohio, lies across Stewart Street to the south of Woodland Cemetery. The school is the home of the U. D. Research Institute, established in 1956. The Institute's areas of research include a number of projects with aerospace applications.

The cemetery gates are open from 7:45 a.m. to 6:00 p.m. in the winter and from 7:45 a.m. to 7:00 p.m. in the summer. The cemetery office is open from 8:00 a.m. to 4:30 p.m. Monday through Friday and from 8:00 a.m. to noon on Saturday. The Mausoleum is open 10:00 a.m. to 4:00 p.m. daily.

Aviation Trail

1. United States Air Force Museum

2. Wright Brothers Memorial

3. Huffman Prairie Flying Field

4. Wright-Patterson Air Force Base

5. Wright State University

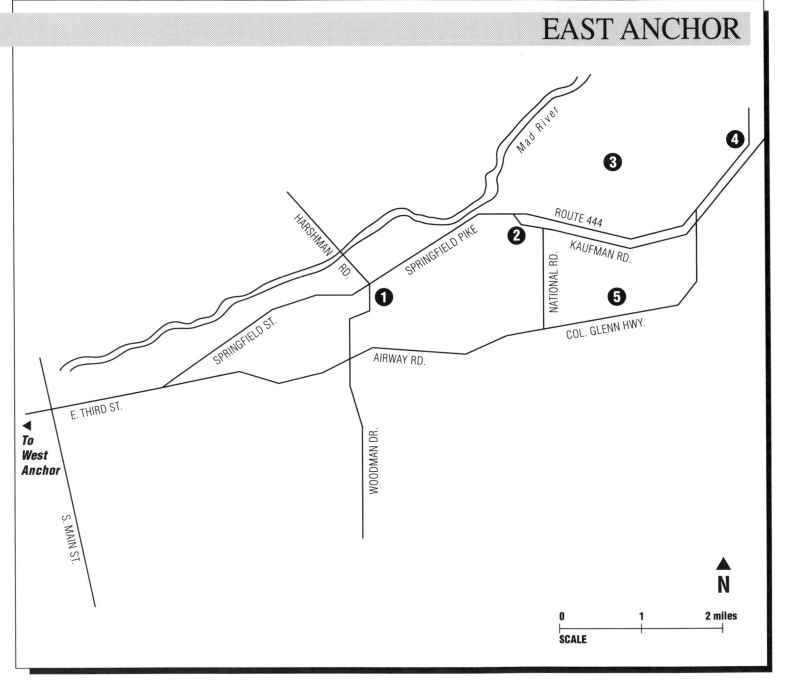

SCALE

0   1   2 miles

N

EAST ANCHOR

The Aviation Trail East Anchor (EA) covers the Wright-Patterson Air Force Base/Wright State University complex, located in eastern Montgomery County, western Greene County and the city of Fairborn.

East Anchor sites include:

- Huffman Prairie, where Wilbur and Orville Wright conducted early flying experiments, operated a flying school and tested Wright Company airplanes,
- The Wright Brothers Memorial on Wright Brothers Hill,
- Wright State University (WSU), with the Wright Brothers Collection, one of the most complete collections of material related to the Wrights in the world,
- The United States Air Force Museum, the largest military aviation museum in the world,
- And Wright-Patterson Air Force Base (W-PAFB), the largest United States Air Force base in the world in terms of personnel.

The East Anchor is the eastern end of the *Pathway to Flight*, the route traveled by the Wright brothers from their home in Dayton's West Side to their flying field at Huffman Prairie. Huffman Prairie is now part of Wright-Patterson Air Force Base, where current research and development projects are laying the groundwork for future aerospace missions undreamed of by Wilbur and Orville Wright when they made the world's first manned powered flight in 1903.

EA 1   United States Air Force Museum
        Springfield Pike at Gate 28B
        Wright-Patterson Air Force Base, Ohio
        45433

The United States Air Force Museum is the largest and oldest military aviation museum in the world. It also is the planned site of the new home of the National Aviation Hall of Fame. The museum contains more than 5,000 items that tell the story of military aviation from man's earliest dreams of flight up to the present space age.

The museum's self-guided tour begins with a display depicting man's earliest dreams of flight as expressed in ancient myths. Among these is the story of Daedalus and his son Icarus, who died when he ignored his father's warning and flew too close to the sun, melting his wings of wax and feathers.

The balloon exhibit describes man's first practical escape from earth's confines, beginning with the first manned flight of a lighter-than-air vehicle, in 1783, a 25-minute, five-mile flight over Paris, France in a hot air balloon developed by the Montgolfier brothers. Balloons became the first United States military aircraft when hydrogen gas balloons were used for observation by both the Union and Confederate forces during the Civil War (1861 to 1865).

The modern aviation age was ushered in by the invention of heavier-than-air aircraft in 1903 when Wilbur and Orville Wright flew their Flyer I at Kitty Hawk, North Carolina on December 17.

The world's first military airplane was a version of the Wrights' Model A, purchased in 1909 by the United States Army Signal Corps. Redesignated Signal Corps Airplane No. 1, the machine was purchased on the assumption its primary function would be for observation, as was the case with military balloons. A replica of the plane is on display in the museum's Wright brothers exhibit.

Although United States military airplanes first saw action in 1916 during the Mexican Punitive Expedition, the first large scale use came during World War I (1914 to 1918). Possessing minimal air-power when it first declared war on Germany in June 1917, the United States decided to adapt the British-designed DeHaviland-4 (DH-4) airplane to American needs. Most of the DH-4s, the only all American-built airplane to see action in World War I, were manufactured by the Dayton Wright Airplane Company (SL 5).

Among the museum's World War I collection are a DeHaviland-4; a Standard J-1 training plane, also manufactured by Dayton Wright; a Curtiss JN-4D Jenny trainer and a Liberty engine, the only American airplane engine manufactured during the war. Foreign World War I airplanes include a replica of a British Sopwith Camel, a restored French Spad VII and a restored Caproni CA 36 bomber.

During the period between World War I and World War II the United States armed forces carried out a number of projects and experiments to increase America's military aviation capability and to expand the role of the airplane. McCook Field (NL 1), in operation from 1917 to 1927, played a leading role in many of these efforts.

Exhibits related to McCook Field include a display about the freefall parachute, which was developed at the field, and an exhibit about the high altitude records set by McCook test pilots.

Among the museum's 1920s and 1930s aircraft are a Verville-Sperry M-1 Messenger, developed at McCook to carry dispatches, and the Loening OA-1A Amphibian *San Francisco*, designed by one-time Wright Company (WA 11) factory manager Grover Loening, one of five OA-1As to make a 22,000-mile Central and South American goodwill tour in 1926-1927.

Other between-the-wars airplanes are a consolidated PT-1 Trusty primary trainer, developed from the Dayton Wright TW-3 airplane; a replica of a Boeing P-26, the first all-metal monoplane produced for the Army Air Corps; and a Boeing B-17G Flying Fortress bomber, the prototype of which was tested at Wright-Patterson Air Force Base (EA 4) in 1935.

At the advent of World War II (1939 to 1945), United States air power again was behind that of the Europeans. In January 1939 the United States had just 500 first-line airplanes compared to 2,000 first-line airplanes in the British Royal Air Force and 4,000 in the German

Luftwaffe. However, determined catch-up efforts during the war made the United States a first-rate air power by the end of the conflict.

The museum's extensive collection of World War II aircraft includes a Northrop P-16C Black Widow, the first United States airplane designed specifically as a night fighter; a Sikorsky R-4B Hoverfly, the world's first production helicopter; and a Bell P-59B Airacomet, the first American jet-propelled airplane, which was used for training but did not see combat during the war.

Other American World War II aircraft include a CG-4A glider manufactured by the Waco Aircraft Company (NL 5), like those used in the D-Day invasion of France on June 6, 1944, and the Boeing B-29 Superfortress *Bockscar*. The *Bockscar* was the airplane from which the second atomic bomb was dropped, on Nagasaki, Japan, August 9, 1945 -- an action that led to the end to World War II with the formal surrender of the Japanese to General Douglas MacArthur on September 2, 1945.

Replica of the first military airplane, a modified Wright Model A purchased by the United States Army in 1909. The replica is an exhibit at the United State Air Force Museum.

Among the foreign World War II aircraft are a German Messerschmitt Me-262 Schwalbe (Swallow), the world's first operational turbojet aircraft, and a British Supermarine Spitfire Mark L.F. XVIE, also used by other Allied countries.

Other World War II exhibits include a model of a German V-1 Buzz Bomb used against England, a Japanese Kugisho Ohka suicide bomb used against United States naval forces, and the casings of *Little Boy* and *Fat Man*, the two atomic bombs dropped on Japan to end the war. Top secret research performed in Dayton by Monsanto Chemical Company produced the critical chemical and metallurgy techniques needed to initiate the atomic explosion in the two bombs.

The jet age arrived with the invention of the jet engine in 1937 by German Hans von Ohain, who became a civilian employee at Wright-Patterson Air Force Base after World War II ended. Hans von Ohain (1912-   ) was inducted into the National Aviation Hall of Fame in 1990.

The museum's jet age collection begins with its Korean War (1950-1953) aircraft. These include a North American F-86D Sabre, the first American swept-wing jet fighter, and a Russian Mikoyan-Gurevich MiG-15 Fagot, flown to South Korea in 1953 by a defecting North Korean pilot and later tested at Wright-Patterson.

Among the Vietnam conflict (1961 to 1973) aircraft are an O-1G Bird Dog, an observation plane manufactured by Cessna Aircraft Company, and a Boeing B-52D Stratofortress, a long-range heavy bomber. Three Stratofortresses were the first jet aircraft to fly nonstop around the world, making the flight in 1957 in less than 45.5 hours with only three in-air refuelings.

Operation Dessert Storm (1990-1991) aircraft include a Fairfield Republic A-10A Thunderbolt II, the first United States Air Force airplane designed specifically for close air support of ground forces.

Experimental and scientific aircraft include a Douglas X-3 Stiletto, first tested in 1952, which was used in high altitude tests at supersonic speeds; a North American X-15A-2, first flown in 1959, with which several pilots reached an altitude above 50 miles, earning an "astronaut" rating; a North American XB-70 Valkyrie, first flown in 1964, which was built to study the aerodynamics and propulsion of large supersonic aircraft and "Tacit Blue," built to test Stealth airplane technology from 1978 to 1985. The museum also has a Stealth bomber.

Other aircraft include three presidential airplanes: the Douglas C-54 *Sacred Cow*, built in 1944 for President Franklin D. Roosevelt, the first president to travel by air while in office; the Douglas VC-119 *Independence*, used by Harry Truman from 1947 to 1953; and the Lockheed VC 121-E Constellation *Columbine III*, President Dwight Eisenhower's personal airplane from 1954 to 1961. The presidential aircraft are displayed in the Annex, two original Wright Field hangars located to the east of the museum's main building. Check at the Information Desk for instructions on how to gain access to the Annex.

The United States missile program dates back to World War I when Charles F. Kettering developed the first guided missile, the *Bug*, at South Field (see SL 4). A replica of the *Bug* is on display in the museum's World War I section. Today, the country's missile program helps maintain the nation's security and supports its space program.

Among the museum's missile collection (on display outside in front of the museum building) are a Martin TM-61A Matador, the first Air Force tactical guided missile, first deployed in 1954; a Chrysler PGM-19 Jupiter, an intermediate range ballistic missile (IRBM), first operational in 1959; a Martin HGM-25A Titan I, a liquid-fueled intercontinental ballistic missile (ICBM), first operational in 1962; and a Boeing LGM-30G Minuteman III, a solid-propellant ICBM, also first operational in 1962.

America entered the space age in 1958 with the launching of the first United States satellite. Since then many military and civilian benefits have accrued from the program, including over 12,000 new products and techniques.

Among the museum's space age exhibits are the Stargazer balloon gondola used in a project established in 1959 to collect space data, a Mercury Spacecraft like the one that made six one-man flights from 1961 to 1963, and a Gemini Spacecraft like the one that made ten two-man flights from 1965 to 1966. Other displays include the Apollo 15 Command Module, one of three components of the Apollo Spacecraft that carried Colonel David R. Scott, Lieutenant Colonel James

B. Irwin and Major Alfred W. Worden, Jr. on a 12-day trip to the moon and back in 1971; and a moon rock collected by Apollo 16 astronauts in 1972.

The United States Air Force Museum dates back to 1923 when a museum to collect technical information was established in a corner of a McCook Field hangar. In 1927 the museum, along with other McCook activities, was moved to Wright Field. There it occupied part of a laboratory (Building 16 in Area B) until 1936 when a new museum building was completed (Building 12 in Area B). Soon after World War II started, the new museum was closed because the space was needed for more vital activities. Upon reopening in 1954, the museum was installed in a former engine overhaul building (Building 89 in Area A). In 1971 the museum moved to its present location on what was once part of Wright Field.

The present museum building was obtained through the efforts of a group of Dayton citizens organized in 1960 as the nonprofit Air Force Museum Foundation. Under the leadership of Eugene Kettering, son of Charles F. Kettering (see SL 4), the Foundation raised over $6,000,000 for the project. The initial building was expanded in 1976. A second hangar component, for the Modern Flight Gallery,

North American XB-70 *Valkyrie* at the United States Air Force Museum. The *Valkyrie*, a 1960s research airplane, could fly at three times the speed of sound. The airplane is now displayed inside in the Modern Flight Gallery.

was added to the rear in 1988. And an IMAX theater, added to the front, was opened in 1991. Now plans are being developed for a third hangar, to be added to the rear, which will have a Cold War Gallery with a missile component.

In addition to acquiring, restoring and maintaining exhibits, the museum operates a Research Division with over 75,000 documents. The division is open to scholars and researchers by appointment only. Hours are weekdays 9:00 a.m to 4:00 p.m.

The museum grounds include a Memorial Park containing statues, plaques and trees dedicated to the memory of individuals, organizations and military units associated with the United States Air Force.

The National Aviation Hall of Fame is scheduled to establish its new home and museum in a separate structure attached to the United States Air Force Museum near the entrance to the Modern Flight Gallery.

Formed in 1962 and chartered by the federal government in 1974, the National Aviation Hall of Fame honors outstanding individuals in the field of aviation at an annual induction ceremony held in Dayton. The first to be inducted were Wilbur and Orville Wright, who were honored in 1962 for inventing the first successful man-carrying powered airplane, first flown on December 17, 1903 at Kitty Hawk, North Carolina.

A flip of a coin and a twist of fate decreed that Orville should be the pilot on that historic flight. Three days earlier the brothers had flipped a coin to determine who should be the first to fly their 1903 Flyer on what they expected to be its first successful test. Wilbur won, but the machine failed to become airborne and was damaged in the attempt. After repairing the plane, a second test was made on December 17. This time it was Orville's turn to act as pilot, and thus it was Orville who piloted the plane on the famous flight. The first flight lasted 12 seconds and covered 120 feet. Altogether, the Wrights made four flights that December 17th before the airplane was severely damaged by a sudden gust of wind, making further tests impossible. The last flight, made by Wilbur, lasted 59 seconds and covered 852 feet.

Man's conquest of the skies progressed rapidly after that first 120-foot flight in 1903. Less than 66 years later, on July 20, 1969, Neil Armstrong, of Wapakoneta, Ohio, became the first human to set foot on the moon. Armstrong now lives it Lebanon, Ohio, a short distance south of Dayton.

The roster of the National Aviation Hall of Fame inductees includes many with a Dayton connection in addition to Wilbur and Orville Wright. Among those associated with the Wrights are:

- Charles Taylor, who made the first airplane engine in the Wright bicycle shop (WA 7),
- Roy Knabenshue, who headed The Wright Company Exhibition Department (CL 6),
- Grover Loening, a prominent airplane designer and manufacturer, who was once factory manager of The Wright Company (WA 11),
- Calbraith "Cal" Rodgers, the first to fly across the continent, who learned to fly at the Wrights' Huffman Prairie flying school (EA 3),
- And Chance Vought, a well-known aircraft designer, who learned to fly at the Wrights' Huffman Prairie flying school.

Inductees associated with McCook Field (NL 1) include:
- John A. Macready, who was co-pilot on the first nonstop flight across the continent and made the first night emergency parachute jump (SL 2) while stationed at the field,
- Donald Douglas, who designed the Douglas World Cruisers used on the first flight around the world, a project in which McCook Field played a prominent role,
- Leigh Wade, a McCook test pilot who piloted one of the airplanes on the first flight around the world,
- George W. Goddard, a pioneer aerial photographer, who headed McCook's photography section,
- Lawrence Sperry, Sr., who was the contractor for the Verville-Sperry Messenger, an airplane developed at McCook, and who once made an unintended parachute landing on the Centre City Office Building (CL 6),
- And Jimmy Doolittle, leader of the Doolittle Raiders who

Orville Wright making the world's first man-carrying, controlled, powered flight, at Kitty Hawk, North Carolina, on December 17, 1903.

dropped the first bombs on Tokyo during World War II, who attended the Engineering School at McCook and later was stationed there.

Others were associated with Wright Field, the successor to McCook and a predecessor of Wright-Patterson Air Force Base (EA 4). These include:

- Benjamin D. Foulois, an early Army pilot who learned to fly through correspondence with Wilbur and Orville Wright, who served as Chief of the Materiel Division in 1929-1930,
- John Atwood, an aircraft engine designer and first president of North American-Rockwell, who started his career in 1928 as a junior engineer at the field,
- Albert F. Hegenberger, who made the first blind solo flight relying entirely on instruments, on May 9, 1932, while stationed at the field,
- George C. Kenney, who was Commander of the Engineering Division at Wright Field in 1940 and Assistant Chief of the Materiel Command in 1941,
- Mark Bradley, former head of the Air Force Logistics Command, who was a test pilot at the field in 1937 and later Chief of the Flight Section,
- Robert A. Hoover, a well-known test pilot, who flight-tested new United States aircraft and flew captured enemy airplanes at the field during World War II,
- And Dominic Gentile, a World War II ace fighter pilot for whom Gentile Air Force Station in Kettering was named, who was a test pilot at Wright Field after the war ended.

Among those associated with the Fairfield Aviation Depot, another predecessor of Wright-Patterson, is:

- Henry "Hap" Arnold, Commander of the Army Air Force during World War II, who was Commander of the Depot in 1929-1930.

Inductees with Wright-Patterson Air Force Base connections include:

- Charles Yeager, the first to fly faster than sound, in 1947, who was stationed at the base after World War II as project pilot for the rocket-powered Bell XS-1 aircraft,
- Albert Boyd, "the test pilot's pilot," who was stationed at the base from 1952 to 1955 as Commander of the Wright Air Development Center,
- Curtis E. LeMay, Air Force Chief of Staff from 1961 to 1965, who was stationed at Air Materiel Headquarters in 1945, served as Vice Commander of the Wright Air Development Division in 1960-1961 and was Vice Commander of the Aeronautical Systems Division in 1961,
- Frank Everest, who served as a test pilot for the Bell X-1 and other aircraft following his release from a Japanese prisoner-of-war camp after the end of World War II,
- Hans P. von Ohain, a German scientist who came to the United States after World War II and was employed at the research laboratories at the base, reaching the rank of Chief Scientist,
- Virgil "Gus" Grissom, who was stationed at the base as a test pilot when he was chosen as an astronaut for the Mercury space program in 1959, and who later was one of three astronauts who died in a tragic fire when they were trapped in the cabin of a spacecraft during a routine land-based simulation test,
- And Robert Rushworth, a test pilot who served at the base as Commander of the 4950th Test Wing and worked in the Directorate of Flight and All-Weather Testing.

Other inductees with Dayton connections are:

- Charles F. Kettering, an inventor and General Motors executive, who was a founder of the Dayton Wright Airplane Company (SL 5),
- William P. Lear, Sr., aircraft manufacturer and developer of the Learjet, who once had an airplane instrument factory north of Dayton (NL 10),
- And Charles A. Lindbergh, the first to fly nonstop across

the Atlantic, who once ferried airplanes for the Waco Aircraft Company (NL 5).

The National Aviation Hall of Fame currently operates out of offices in the Dayton Convention and Exhibition Center at the southeast corner of Main and Fifth Streets in downtown Dayton.

The United States Air Force Museum is open 9:00 a.m. to 5:00 p.m. seven days a week except for New Year's Day, Thanksgiving and Christmas. Admission is free.

EA 2   Wright Brothers Memorial
        Wright Brothers Hill
        Kaufman Road and Route 444
        Wright-Patterson Air Force Base, Ohio
            45433

The Wright Brothers Memorial honors Wilbur and Orville Wright for their original aeronautical research and "further development of the aeroplane … which established aviation as one of the great forward steps in human progress." The memorial stands in a park on top of Wright Brothers Hill, overlooking the Huffman Prairie flying field (EA 3) where the brothers conducted many of their early flying experiments.

The memorial and the 20-acre landscaped park in which it is located were designed by the well-known Olmstead Brothers, Landscape Architects, of Brookline, Massachusetts. The shaft and base of the memorial are made of marble quarried near Kitty Hawk, North Carolina, where Orville Wright made the world's first powered man-carrying flight on December 17, 1903. Earth from the site of the Wright brothers' first hangar at Huffman Prairie, erected in 1904, has been incorporated in the ground beneath the memorial.

A plaque on the low stone wall encircling the terrace sur-rounding the memorial contains the names of 119 early flyers who were taught to fly at the Wrights' Huffman Prairie flying school. Arrows embedded on the top of the wall point to two nearby landmarks: the white cement model that marks the site of the Wrights' first hangar at Huffman Prairie, and Wright Field, the successor to McCook Field (NL 1), which borders on Wright Brothers Hill to the south. Wright Field is now part of Wright-Patterson Air Force Base (EA 4).

The Wright Brothers Memorial was dedicated in the presence of Orville Wright and other dignitaries on August 19, 1940, Orville's 69th birthday. The Miami Conservancy District provided the land; the National Park Service provided Civilian Conservation Corps (CCC) labor; and the Wilbur and Orville Wright Memorial Commission, under the leadership of Colonel Edward A. Deeds (see SL 3), developed the plans and provided the funds.

The citizens of Dayton first proposed a Wright memorial in 1912, shortly after Wilbur's death. At that time the recommendation was to erect two Greek columns at Huffman Prairie in Wilbur's honor, a proposal that never materialized. Later, a portion of the funds raised to purchase land to replace McCook Field was set aside to build a memorial honoring both brothers. Although Wright Field, which replaced McCook, opened in 1927, the plans for the memorial were not agreed to until 1939.

The world was slow to recognize the accomplishments of Wilbur and Orville Wright. Many Americans, convinced that human flight was impossible, refused to believe the stories of their early flying exploits. On the other hand, Europeans recognized the reality of flight, but believed no American was capable of approaching the accomplishments of their experimenters. The Wrights' first widespread acclaim came during their 1908-1909 trip to Europe, five years after their first flight and three years after developing their first practical airplane, the Flyer III.

The first Wright European flights, made by Wilbur at Hunaudieres Race Course at Le Mans, France, August 8 to 13, 1908, caused a sensation as they clearly demonstrated the superiority of the Wright machine over European efforts. Before these flights, Brazilian Alberto

Left to right: Edward P. Warner, Civil Aeronautics Authority; Captain Kenneth L. Whiting, U. S. Navy; Orville Wright and General Henry H. Arnold, U. S. Army; at the dedication of the Wright Brothers Memorial, August 19, 1940.

Santos Dumont had been credited as the first to fly based on a 721-foot flight in a Paris suburb on November 12, 1906, over a year after the Wrights had attained a flight of more than 24 miles on October 5, 1905 in their Flyer III.

Later European demonstrations included flights by Wilbur at Camp d'Auvours, Le Mans from August 21, 1908 to January 2, 1909; at Pont-Long, Pau, France from February 3 to March 20, 1909; and at Centocelle Flying Field, Rome, Italy from April 15 to 27, 1909; as well as flights by Orville at Tempelhof Field, Berlin, Germany from August 30 to September 18, 1909 and Bornstedt Field, Potsdam, Germany from September 29 to October 15, 1909.

The Wrights received many European awards and honors as a result of these demonstrations. Among these were certificates and gold medals recognizing the brothers as the inventors of the airplane and various prizes attesting to their flying skills. Upon their return from Europe in May 1909, America, too, showered the Wrights with numerous gold medals and awards in recognition of their outstanding achievements. And a national monument at Kitty Hawk, North Carolina, dedicated November 19, 1932, commemorates "the conquest of the air by the brothers Wilbur and Orville Wright." The monument, on Kill Devil Hill, marks the sand dunes where the Wrights conducted their early flying experiments from 1900 to 1903.

While preparing the ground for the Dayton memorial, six prehistoric Indian mounds were discovered. Built by early inhabitants of the Miami Valley, the Mound Builders, the mounds served as burial grounds and probably also as observation posts. An arrow embedded in the top of the low stone wall encircling the monument's terrace points out their location. Based on their presence, Wright Brothers Hill is listed on the National Register of Historic Places.

Wright Brothers Hill provides a panoramic view of the Mad River and Huffman Dam (see EA 3). A cut on the north face of the hill is a noted fossil-hunting area.

The Wright Brothers Memorial is open 8:00 a.m. to 8:00 p.m. daily.

EA 3   Huffman Prairie Flying Field
         Wright-Patterson Air Force Base, Ohio
         45433

Huffman Prairie, the world's first flying field, was the scene of Wilbur and Orville Wright's early flying experiments, the location of their first permanent flying school, and later part of the United States Army's Wilbur Wright Field. Sometimes referred to as the Simms Station field because of its location near that stop on the Dayton-Springfield, Ohio interurban traction line, Huffman Prairie is now part of Wright-Patterson Air Force Base (EA 4).

The Huffman Prairie field was established in the spring of 1904 to test the Wright brothers' second machine, the Flyer II. (The Wrights' first flying machine, the Flyer I, was irreparably damaged by a gust of wind after only one day of tests on December 17, 1903 at Kitty Hawk, North Carolina.)

During their first season at Huffman Prairie, the Wrights made 105 starts between May 26 and December 9, 1904, attaining a total flying time of 49 minutes. On September 20 Wilbur flew the world's first complete circle in an airplane, an event witnessed by Amos I. Root of Medina, Ohio. Root later wrote the first published eyewitness account of the Wrights' achievements, which appeared in the January 1, 1905 issue of his magazine, *Gleanings in Bee Culture*.

The article begins, "Dear Friends, I have a wonderful story to tell you -- a story that in some respects outrivals the Arabian Nights fables..."

During the 1904 season the Wrights also developed a new launching system using a derrick and weight, sometimes called a catapult. First used on September 7, the device consisted of a 1,600 pound weight attached to the airplane by ropes and a pulley, a derrick and a short launching rail. Dropping the weight from the top of the derrick sent the plane rolling down the launching rail until the machine gained enough momentum to take off at the end of the track after the rope was released from the machine. The system was developed after the brothers found the 60-foot starting rail used at Kitty Hawk impractical at the new smaller field where the winds were much lighter and the terrain bumpy.

The Flyer II was dismantled in 1905 and some of its parts used to construct the Flyer III.

The Flyer III made 50 flights at Huffman Prairie between June 23 and October 16, 1905. The longest, on October 5, covered more than 24 miles in just under 40 minutes. The Flyer III was the world's first practical airplane. Able to bank, turn, circle and make figure eights, the machine also was the first capable of sustained flight. The 1905 flights, flown in circles around the small field, were witnessed by a number of relatives, friends and others, including newsmen from *The Dayton Journal* and the *Dayton Daily News*. In an October 5, 1905 article, the *News* reported that the Wrights were making sensational flights every day.

At the end of the 1905 season the brothers stored their Flyer III and did no more flying until 1908, to prevent others from learning their secrets while they waited for approval of their patent application and made arrangements to market their invention. Their first patent application, filed March 23, 1903, was approved May 22, 1906. The restored Flyer III is on exhibit at Carillon Historical Park (SL 1).

The brothers first attempted to interest the United States government in their invention early in 1905 when Wilbur contacted Dayton congressman Robert M. Nevin, who suggested they write a letter he could show to President Taft. This and succeeding efforts failed to produce results until 1907, when the United States Signal Corps advertised for bids on a military heavier-than-air-machine on December 23. The Wrights' bid to provide a flying machine for $25,000 was accepted by the War Department on February 8, 1908, subject to meeting specifications.

After receiving the contract, the Wrights modified their 1905 Flyer to meet the government's requirements. As modified, the machine could carry two people sitting upright, rather than one person lying prone as before. Then, in order to regain their flying skills, the brothers returned to Kitty Hawk where they made 22 flights between May 6 and 14. On the last day, they carried a passenger for the first time. At the end of that day, the plane was damaged in an accident.

Orville, left, and Wilbur Wright at Huffman Prairie in 1904.

At the end of these flights, the brothers parted company. Wilbur sailed for Paris on May 21 to conduct flying demonstrations in Europe, in a machine shipped abroad in 1907 but never uncrated. Orville returned to Dayton to build a new machine for the Signal Corps, which he demonstrated at Ft. Myer, near Washington, D. C., later that year.

The demonstrations at Ft. Myer were cut short when Orville's plane crashed on September 17. Orville was injured in the accident and his passenger, Lieutenant Thomas E. Selfridge, was killed -- the first airplane fatality.

Upon resumption of the tests in June 1909, this time with both brothers present, Orville met the Signal Corps requirement for an airplane that could be quickly and easily assembled and could remain aloft for at least one hour while carrying two people. And he exceeded the 40-miles-per-hour speed requirement by averaging 42 miles per hour to earn a $5,000 bonus.

At the end of 1909 Wilbur and Orville formed The Wright Company (see WA 10) to manufacture their invention. Several months later they returned to Huffman Prairie to set up a flying school and to test Wright Company airplanes. The school opened on May 10, 1910 and the first test of a Wright Company airplane was on May 21. Another highlight of that season was the world's first commercial flight, on November 7, from Huffman Prairie to Columbus, Ohio (see WA 10).

The Huffman Prairie school was the Wrights' first permanent flying school, although previously they had trained pilots at various temporary locations in the United States and Europe.

Among those who learned to fly at the Huffman Prairie school were Lieutenant Henry H. Arnold, later Commander of the U. S. Army Air Force during World War II; Captain Roy A. Brown, of the Canadian Royal Air Force, who was credited with shooting down the German World War I ace known as the Red Baron: Griffith Brewer, the first Englishman to fly in an airplane; Cal P. Rodgers, who made the first flight across the continent (see SL 8) and three women: Rose Dugan, Mrs. Richberg Hornsby and Marjorie Stinson. According to The Wright Company's catalog, tuition at the school was $500 (with

Wright airplane with derrick and weight launching mechanism at Pau, France in 1909.

no fee for "breakage") for a seven-to-ten-day course of individual instruction, including four hours flying time in a dual-control Wright Model B.

The Huffman Prairie field was closed in 1916, about a year after Orville sold The Wright Company.

In 1917 Huffman Prairie became part of Wilbur Wright Field, established to train Army pilots, armorers and aircraft mechanics for World War I. The area is now part of Wright-Patterson Air Force Base.

The Huffman Prairie field, about 100 acres, originally was a pasture on the farm of Torrance Huffman, a Dayton bank president, who allowed the Wrights free use of the land provided they did not disturb his livestock. One of the field's attractions was its easy accessibility from the brothers' Dayton home via the Dayton-Springfield interurban line, which had a stop at nearby Simms Station.

The Wright Company hangar at Huffman Prairie. The company tested airplanes and conducted a flying school here from 1910 to 1916.

During the years they were at Huffman Prairie, the Wrights built three wooden hangars: in 1904 for the Flyer II, in 1905 for the Flyer III and in 1910 for their flying school. A white cement model, visible from Wright Brothers Hill (EA 2), marks the site of the 1904 hangar. A replica of the 1905 hangar, along with a model of the derrick, or catapult, they used for starting their airplane, has been erected across from the 1904 marker. The site of the 1910 hangar has been identified by a 1990 archeological study. (The 1910 hangar, which had deteriorated over the years, was demolished in the early 1940s.)

The Wrights' experimental flights were all made within the confines of the flying field by flying around in circles about 40 feet off the ground. This historic circuit has been recreated by a one-mile

mowed path, which includes numbered posts keyed to an interpretive guidebook that describes significant sites along the way. The guidebook is available by the replica of the 1905 hangar. Flags in stonework bases mark the boundaries of the flying field.

A patch of the original prairie, discovered by naturalists in 1985, lies adjacent to the flying field. Now returned to its natural state, it is being maintained through a nuturing of native prairie grasses and other plants. This area has been designated a State Natural Landmark.

The Huffman Prairie Flying Field is one of the four scattered sites in the Dayton Aviation Heritage National Historical Park (see WA 3). It is listed on the National Register of Historic Places and is a National Historic Landmark.

Wright flying school student Marjorie Stinson at Huffman Prairie in 1914. The airplane is a Wright Model B with dual controls.

Today, Huffman Prairie lies in the retarding basin behind Huffman Dam, one of five dams created as part of the Miami Conservancy District flood control system developed after the disastrous 1913 Dayton flood. The system was designed and constructed under the direction of pioneer hydraulic engineer Arthur E. Morgan, later president of Antioch College in nearby Yellow Springs, Ohio from 1920 to 1936.

The present-day city of Fairborn, Ohio is a consequence of the creation of the Huffman Dam retarding basin. Chartered in 1950, the city was formed by the merger of two adjacent villages, Fairfield and Osborn. Originally located on land designated for the retarding basin, Osborn was moved in its entirety in 1921 two and one-half miles east to a new site next to Fairfield. Until the 1950 merger, a single street separated the two towns: Fairfield to the east and Osborn to the west, each with its own municipal structure. The name of Fairborn is a combination of the names of the two original villages.

Huffman Prairie Flying Field is open to the public. For information about how to gain access through Wright-Patterson Air Force Base telephone 937-257-5535. Admission is free.

EA 4   Wright-Patterson Air Force Base
Springfield Pike/Route 444
Wright-Patterson Air Force Base, Ohio
45433

Wright-Patterson Air Force Base (W-PAFB) is the largest United States Air Force base in the world in terms of personnel and the largest employer in the Miami Valley. Covering approximately 8,000 acres, the base houses over 100 organizations, has an annual payroll of more than $900,000,000 and employs about 25,600 (8,500 military, 13,700 civilians and 3,400 contractors or persons who work under contract services.)

Wright-Patterson activities include research and development and logistics management, the base's two major missions, as well as flight operations, advanced education, medical services, reserve readiness and various other defense-related activities.

Wright-Patterson research and development organizations include the Aeronautical Systems Center and its Wright Laboratory, which are part of Air Force Materiel Command (AFMC), the National Air Intelligence Center and a major portion of Armstrong Laboratory. The headquarters of AFMC, one of ten major Air Force Commands, also is located on the base. AFMC employs the majority of the Air Force's scientists and engineers and is responsible for the research, development, test, acquisition, delivery and logistics support of all the service's weapon systems.

Aeronautical Systems Center (ASC), the base's host and largest unit, traces its origin to McCook Field's (NL 1) Engineering Division. ASC oversees the development and acquisition of all Air Force aeronautical systems and equipment, including fighters, bombers, transports, tankers, air-to-surface missiles, simulators, trainers, airplane engines, unmanned aerial vehicles, and reconnaissance and electronic warfare systems.

ASC's Wright Laboratory develops advanced technologies for weapon systems and other equipment. The laboratory's research is conducted through six major technology directorates, five of which are located at the base. The five at the base are:

- Aero Propulsion and Power, which focuses on air-breathing propulsion and airborne power technology, including fuels and lubricants, turbine engines, and high-performance, high-Mach, air-breathing propulsion applications;
- Avionics, which conducts research and development in the fields of offensive sensors (such as radar and forward-looking infrared), weapon delivery systems, reconnaissance, electronic warfare, navigation, communications, avionics integration and electronic devices in microelectronics and electro-optics;
- Flight Dynamics, which conducts the full spectrum of flight vehicle research, including aircraft structures, vehi-

Lieutenant Frank Stuart Patterson, for whom Patterson Field was named, in a portrait by Jane Reese, noted Dayton photographer. Patterson was killed in a flying accident at Wilbur Wright Field in 1918.

cle subsystems such as landing gear, flight control, and aeromechanics;

- Manufacturing Technology, which is the focal point for planning and executing an integrated manufacturing program across the Air Force, with an emphasis on the need to design for productibility, quality and life-cycle costs;
- Materials, which researches new materials and processes, with a current emphasis on materials for thermal protection, metallic and nonmetallic structures, aerospace propulsion, electromagnetics and electronics, and laser-hardened systems.

The National Air Intelligence Center (NAIC) is the primary source of foreign aerospace intelligence for the Department of Defense. The Center assesses current and projected foreign aerospace capabilities, develops targeting and mission-planning intelligence materials and evaluates evolving technologies of potential adversaries. NAIC's roots go back to the Foreign Data Section of the Airplane Engineering Department at McCook Field.

The Armstrong Laboratory's Crew Systems Directorate conducts research and development and provides field support to integrate human operators with weapon systems and to obtain optimum human combat performance.

The Air Force Material Command (AFMC) Headquarters is responsible for providing the Air Force's operational units with the best possible aircraft, missiles and support equipment. It also provides support to other United States military forces, as well as allies, and conducts research, development, testing and evaluation of satellites, boosters, space probes and associated systems for NASA projects. Other major AFMC units located at the base, in addition to ASC and the Armstromg Laboratory unit are:

- AFMC Law Center, which provides legal advice to various commanders and staff throughout the Air Force, reviews final decisions of all Air Force contracting officers and represents the Air Force in litigation before the Armed Services Board of Contract Appeals;
- Air Force Security Assistance Center, which manages

contracts for foreign military sales, provides support for an inventory of a total of more than 11,000 aircraft located in more than 80 countries, and participates in other security assistance programs.

Four other unrelated major units are located at the base. These are the Air Force Institute of Technology, the Wright-Patterson Medical Center, the 445th Airlift Wing and the 88th Air Base Wing.

The Air Force Institute of Technology (AFIT) is a descendant of McCook Field's Air Service Engineering School. Today the Institute includes four resident schools and the office of Civilian Institution Programs, which manages graduate degree programs and continuing education courses for Air Force personnel at various off-base schools and other institutions. The four resident schools, which provide graduate courses and continuing professional education programs, are the Graduate School of Engineering; School of Systems and Logistics; School of Civil Engineering and Morale, Welfare, Recreation and Services; and the Graduate School of Logistics and Acquisition Management.

The Wright-Patterson Medical Center provides medical services to a seven-state region. In addition to a hospital that provides patient care, the Center participates in the training of medical professionals, including physician training in cooperation with the nearby Wright State University (EA 5) Medical School.

The 445th Airlift Wing of the United States Air Force Reserve is trained to provide strategic worldwide transport as needed, such as aeromedical evacuation of personnel as well as equipment. Recent activities have included mercy missions to countries in Africa and a ground support mission to Bosnia.

The 88th Air Base Wing, a unit of Aeronautical Systems Center (ASC), provides services similar to those provided by the government of a city. These include maintaining the physical facilities of the base; providing police and fire protection, transportation services and recreational facilites and programs; handling payroll and personnel records; and operating the runway complex. The Wing also operates an aircraft tire storage and distribution depot, manages a fleet of C-21As and provides other specialized services.

The United States Air Force Museum (EA 1), the Wright Brothers Memorial (EA 2) and Huffman Prairie Flying Field (EA 3), all described separately, also are located on base property.

Wright-Patterson Air Force Base was formed through the merger of Wright Field and Patterson Field on January 13, 1948, six months after the creation of a separate air service, the United States Air Force. Wright Field and Patterson Field, in turn, had grown out of several earlier organizations starting with Wilbur Wright Field and the Fairfield Aviation General Supply Depot, both formed during World War I.

Wilbur Wright Field was established by the Army in May 1917 to train pilots, aircraft mechanics and armorers, and to conduct aircraft firearms tests. The field was named for Wilbur, who died in 1912, the older of the two brothers who invented the airplane. Located on approximately 2,000 acres leased by the federal government from the Miami Conservancy District, the field included Huffman Prairie, where the Wrights tested their early airplanes and later had a flying school. Although none of the original operations buildings on Wilbur Wright Field remain, the Commander's residence is still standing. Currently the home of the ASC Commander, it is referred to as the Foulois House (Building 88, Area C).

The Fairfield Aviation General Supply Depot was established by the Army in June 1917 to supply the Signal Corps aviation schools in the eastern United States, including nearby Wilbur Wright Field. The depot was located on 40 acres, purchased for $8,000, near the town of Fairfield. After the end of World War I, the depot was expanded and renamed the Fairfield Intermediate Air Depot, later changed to the Fairfield Air Depot Reservation. The first building (Building 1, Area C) is still standing, as is a house built in 1841 (Building 8, Area C) that was the residence of several commanders, including Henry H. "Hap" Arnold, who, when a major, served as the depot commander from 1929 to 1930. Arnold later was Commander of the United States Army Air Force (USAAF) during World War II. Now called Arnold House, the renovated building currently contains exhibits, offices and meeting rooms.

Wright Field, named for both Wilbur and Orville Wright, was

Aerial view of Wright Field in 1932. The light colored building to the left of the semi-circular drive in the center of the picture is now part of Building 16, Area B at Wright-Patterson Air Force Base.

Douglas XB-19 at the company's plant in Santa Monica, California. The World War II bomber was tested at Wright Field in the 1940s.

dedicated October 12, 1927 in the presence of Orville and high government officials. Built as a replacement for McCook Field, the new field covered approximately 4,500 acres, including Wilbur Wright Field.

Wright Field came about through the efforts of the Dayton Air Service Committee, led by Frederick B. Patterson, son of National Cash Register Company founder John H. Patterson. The committee raised funds to purchase land east of Dayton, which it then gave to the federal government as an inducement to keep McCook's research and development activities in the area rather than have them move else-where as had been proposed. The committee raised the funds in 1922 in just three days, collecting contributions from nearly 600 individuals, families and businesses.

The first two main Wright Field buildings (Buildings 11 and 16, Area B) are still standing. A flagpole and commemorative plaque erected in connection with a Wright Field rededication ceremony on Oct. 12, 1984 are in the plaza between Buildings 14 and 16 in Area B.

Patterson Field, established July 6, 1931, was named for Lieutenant Frank Stuart Patterson, son of John H. Patterson's brother, Frank. Lieutenant Patterson and Lieutenant Leroy A. Swan lost their lives in an airplane accident at Wilbur Wright Field on June 19, 1918 while flying a DeHaviland-4 (see SL 5) to test the synchronization of a machine gun with the airplane's propellers. The field, located on about 3,800 acres in the retarding basin behind Huffman Dam, included the areas once occupied by the two original organizations, Fairfield Aviation General Supply Depot and Wilbur Wright Field. (Wilbur Wright Field had previously been a part of Wright Field.)

The base has a rich history of contributions to aerospace research and development, starting with research areas originally initiated at McCook Field that were continued after the move to Wright Field (see NL 1). Later, Wright Field played a prominent role during World War II, including the testing of new combat aircraft. Among these was the B-19 bomber, for which a special inclined runway was built. (The runway later was used for soapbox derby races, a youth sport that originated in Dayton.)

Among post-World War II activities were Project Bluebook, which gathered data about unidentified flying objects from 1948 to 1967; development of the spacesuit worn by Ohioan John Glenn in 1962 when he became the first American to orbit the earth; and operation of a nuclear engineering center from 1964 to 1970.

In 1995 Wright-Patterson Air Force Base took on an entirely new role when it was asked to host the Proximity Peace Talks to try to end the long-running war in the Balkans. The talks, carried out from November 1 to 27, brought together the leaders of the three warring factions, Serbia, Croatia and Bosnia, in a secure environment with a minimum of distractions that the planners felt would be most conducive to a positive outcome. On November 27 an agreement was reached, which subsequently became known as the Dayton peace agreement.

Today, Wright-Patterson is engaged in a major construction program to update its research, development and acquisition facilities. And the base is moving toward sharing some of the results of its research with the civilian community under a technology transfer program.

Wright-Patterson Air Force Base is not open to the public.

EA 5   Wright State University
3640 Colonel Glenn Highway
Dayton, Ohio 45435

Wright State University (WSU), named for Wilbur and Orville Wright, owns an extensive collection of aviation research material, including the Wright Brothers Collection. The material is located in the Archives and Special Collections Division at the University's Paul Laurence Dunbar Library.

The Wright Brothers Collection includes aviation books, photographs and original documents, as well as a number of trophies and medals awarded to the brothers in recognition of their achievements. One of the trophies, the *Coupe Michelin pour L'Aviation*, for the longest flight of 1908, is on display in a special case resting on a stand made of bricks from Orville Wright's laboratory (WA 6). The trophy was awarded to Wilbur for a flight of over 123 kilometers at d'Auvours, France on December 31, 1908. The competition was sponsored by Edward and Andre Michelin, who commissioned sculptor Paul Roussel to design the trophy.

The WSU collection of Wright medals includes a number of duplicates because on many occasions each brother was presented an identical award. Among the medals are the City of Dayton, State of Ohio and Congressional gold medals presented to the brothers during the 1909 Dayton homecoming celebration (described under WA 2), a gold medal awarded by the Aero Club of America in 1910 and the gold medals presented during their 1908-1909 trip to Europe. Originally bequeathed to the Dayton Art Institute by Orville Wright in 1948, the medals were acquired by WSU in 1979.

Wright State is a major resource for aviation scholars and researchers throughout the world. Among foreign visitors who have made use of the school's archives are Bruce Winder of New Zealand and Countess Maria Caproni of Italy. Winder researched the design of early Wright gliders, then built a reproduction of the 1902 model, which he flew at a spot in New Zealand that duplicated conditions at Kitty Hawk, North Carolina where the Wrights flew the original. The Countess, daughter of Italian airplane designer Giovanni Caproni, researched the Wrights' activities in Italy for the Caproni museum. Almost every major publication about the Wright brothers includes pictures from the WSU collection of over 3,500 Wright-related photographs.

The Wright Brothers Collection by Patrick B. Nolan and John A. Zamonski lists the materials in the WSU collection. In addition to the photographs, these include technical books, journals and pamphlets; manuscripts and records; Bishop Milton Wright's papers and genealogical materials; and recognitions and memorabilia. The collection, with more than 6,000 items, is one of the most complete in the world.

The major portion of the collection came to the University through the children of Wilbur and Orville Wright's brother Lorin: Milton Wright, Horace Wright, Ivonette Wright Miller and Leontine Wright Jameson. Under Orville's will, the executors of his estate were to select a suitable institution as a repository for the Wright papers. The institution selected, the Library of Congress, surveyed the material and chose about 100 publications, 303 glass negatives taken by the brothers and their 1900 to 1910 correspondence with Octave Chanute. The remainder of the material was acquired from the estate by the Lorin Wright family, which donated it to Wright State in 1975. Since then other items from various sources have been added, including a rare motion picture film of part of Wilbur's 1908 flight that won him the Michelin Trophy.

The WSU aviation collection also includes the papers of Charles Furnas, the Wright mechanic who was their first airplane passenger; William G. Lambert, second ranking World War I ace with 22 victories; Fred Marshall, an aviation writer; and Clayton Brukner, cofounder of the Waco Aircraft Company (NL 5).

Wright State University was started in 1964 as a joint operation of Miami University, Oxford, Ohio and The Ohio State University, Columbus, Ohio. Conceived as a living memorial to the achievements of Wilbur and Orville Wright, the school was named Wright State University upon being declared an independent institution in 1967. The campus contains more than 600 acres, part of which was donated by Wright-Patterson Air Force Base (EA 4).

Wright State's academic areas cover business administration, education and human services, science and engineering, and medicine, including an aerospace medical program. A special aspect of the University are provisions for handicapped students that from the beginning have been integrated into the design of all campus facilities.

The Archives and Special Collections Division at the Wright State University Paul Laurence Dunbar Library is open to the public. Open hours during the fall to spring academic terms are 8:30 a.m. to 5:00 p.m. Monday through Friday; 7:00 to 10:00 p.m. Tuesday and Wednesday and 2:00 to 5:00 p.m. Sunday. During academic breaks and the summer term, the evening and Sunday hours are eliminated.

The Congressional gold medal awarded to the Wright brothers during Dayton's homecoming celebration in 1909. The medal is one of a collection of Wright medals owned by Wright State University.

Aviation Trail

1. McCook Field Site

2. First Emergency Freefall Parachute Jump Landing Site

3. Former McGuire Products Company Factory

4. Former International Flare and Signal Company Office

5. Former WACO Aircraft Company Factory

6. WACO Aircraft Museum

7. Hartzell Propeller Inc.

8. McCauley Accessory Division

9. Former Aeroproducts Factory

10. Former Lear Avia, Inc. Factory

11. Dayton International Airport

12. Brookville Community Museum

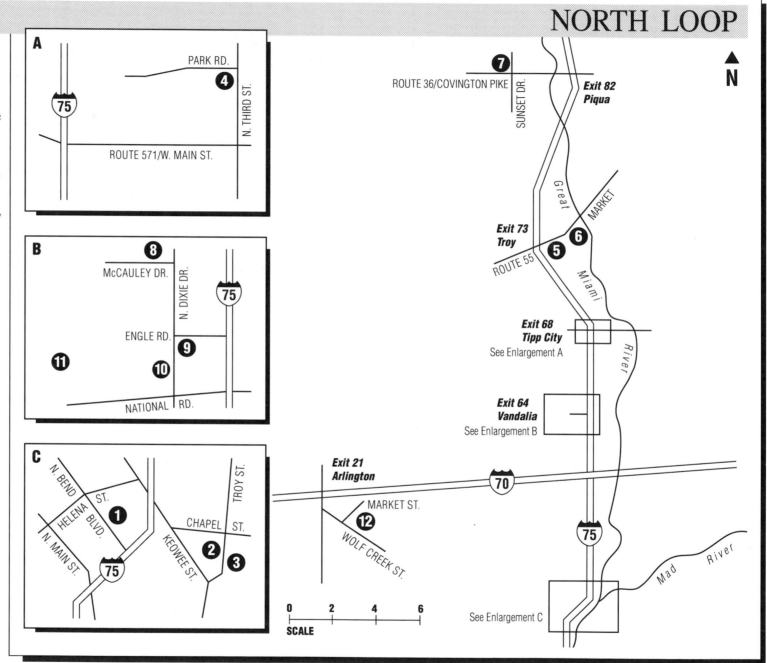

NORTH LOOP

The Aviation Trail North Loop (NL) covers north Dayton and the northern communities of Tipp City, Troy, Piqua, Vandalia and Brookville. North Loop sites related to current or former aviation manufacturers include:

- The Waco Aircraft Company, the country's largest producer of civil aircraft in the 1920s and 1930s,
- The WACO Aircraft Museum, with displays of Waco memorabilia,
- Hartzell Propeller Inc., manufacturer of airplane propellers,
- Cessna McCauley Accessory Division, manufacturer of airplane propellers,
- General Motors Aeroproducts Division, manufacturer of Aeroprop propellers during World War II,
- Lear Avia, Inc., manufacturer of various aircraft instruments during the 1930s and 1940s.
- International Flare and Signal Company, manufacturer of the first electronically-controlled airplane flare, developed during World War II,
- And McGuire Products Company, producer of the Little Robot automatic pilot in the 1930s.

Other North Loop sites are:

- The former location of McCook Field, the first United States military aviation research and development center and the birthplace of the freefall parachute,
- The landing site of the first emergency freefall parachute jump,
- Brookville Community Museum, with an exhibit about early balloonist Warren Rasor,
- And Dayton International Airport, home of the annual United States Air and Trade Show.

NL 1 McCook Field Site
North Bend Boulevard
Dayton, Ohio 45404

McCook Field, called the "Cradle of Aviation," was the first United States military aviation research center. The field was located along the Great Miami River near downtown Dayton from 1917 to 1927.

Established during World War I to support the United States war effort, McCook's greatest impact came during the post-war years when its activities were largely responsible for the 1920 to 1925 period being called America's "golden era of exploration and records" in aviation. McCook's contributions included:

- Development of the modern freefall parachute,
- Development of aerial photography,
- High altitude experiments that made high altitude flying feasible,
- Establishment of test airways and the development of airway equipment,
- Design and testing of aircraft,
- Propeller and engine improvements,
- Development of commercial applications,
- And the operation of an aviation information clearinghouse.

The field also played a major role in several landmark flights, including the first nonstop flight across the continent and the first flight around the world.

The first nonstop flight across the continent, described under CL 7, was conceived, planned and carried out by McCook personnel. During the record-making trip on May 2-3, 1923, McCook test pilots Lieutenants John A. Macready and Oakley G. Kelly covered 2,470 miles in 26 hours and 50 minutes.

McCook was the logistics center for the first flight around the world, in 1924, and three of those making the trip were from the field: pilots Leigh Wade and Erik Nelson and mechanic Jack Harding. The

The main hangar at McCook Field in 1927.

trip was made in four Douglas World Cruisers, two-seat open cockpit biplanes equipped with reconditioned Liberty engines left over from World War I.

Only two of the planes, the *New Orleans*, piloted by Nelson, and the *Chicago*, completed the trip, covering 26,445 miles in a little more than 360 hours flying time over a period of five and one-half months between April 6 and September 28. Planning challenges for the pioneer trip ranged from complex political negotiations for permission to overfly or land at foreign countries to the selection and stockpiling of fuel, spare parts and other supplies at strategic fields along the route. The trip demonstrated the practicality of the airplane and showed the feasibility of flight over land and water under varying weather and geographic conditions.

Leigh Wade (1896-   ) was inducted into the National Aviation Hall of Fame (see EA 1) in 1974.

McCook's role in the development of the modern freefall parachute, first tested by a human in 1919, makes Dayton the birthplace of the parachute as well as the birthplace of aviation. The development of the parachute is described under the landing site of the first emergency freefall parachute jump (NL 2), made by McCook test pilot Lieutenant Harold R. Harris in 1922. The first night emergency freefall parachute jump was made by Lieutenant John A. Macready in 1924 (SL 2).

McCook's pioneering aerial photography activities were under the direction of Lieutenant George W. Goddard, who took the first night aerial photograph in 1925. Goddard also developed the first strip camera, which made one continuous picture, and later, at Wright Field (see EA 4), directed the development of the panoramic camera. George W. Goddard (1889-1987) was inducted into the National Aviation Hall of Fame in 1976.

Among other McCook photography firsts was the first aerial photographic survey of the entire country, made in the summer of 1923 by McCook pilots Lieutenants John A. Macready and Albert W Stevens.

McCook pilots conducted numerous high altitude experiments during which a number of records were set. One such experiment was a flight on February 27, 1920 made by Lieutenant Rudolph W. "Shorty" Schroeder in an open cockpit LePere biplane. Schroeder climbed to a record high of 33,113 feet, but in the process almost lost his life. Although his eyes froze shut in the 67-degrees-below-zero temperature and he lost consciousness due to a lack of oxygen plus carbon monoxide poisoning from the exhaust, Schroeder miraculously recovered his senses at 3,000 feet just long enough to set the airplane in a glide into the field, where he was found at the end of the runway sitting unconscious in the cockpit of his plane. Schroeder also was the first person to make a night flight and later became an expert in airplane safety, promoting the use of redundant systems in commercial aircraft.

McCook's high altitude experiments led to the development of the first pressurized airplane cabin and the first pressurized suit, technologies that made high altitude flying feasible. (Without these aids people are apt to become unconscious and die at altitudes above 20,000 feet.) The pressurized airplane, first flown by Lieutenant Harris on June 8, 1921, initially was developed to provide a stable environment for cameras, with its value to humans emerging later.

McCook's contributions to airway development included the establishment of a model airway between Dayton and Washington, D. C.; the operation of the first night airway, between Dayton and Columbus, Ohio; and the development of routing aids. The model air-

First around-the-world flyers at McCook Field in 1924. Left to right: Major J. F. Curry, McCook's Commanding Officer; Lieutenant E. H. Smith; Lieutenant H. H. Ogden; McCook test pilots Lieutenant Erik Nelson and Lieutenant Leigh Wade; McCook mechanic Lieutenant Jack Harding and Lieutenant Leslie P. Arnold.

way, first opened in February 1921, was operated on a regular schedule to study how flight could be made a practical method of transportation, to train cross-country pilots and to test air navigation instruments. The night airway, inaugurated in July 1923 and also operated on a regular schedule, used rotating beacons to mark its lighted 80-mile route, an innovation that greatly expanded the amount of flying that could be done in a day. (Previously, pilots were forced to stop flying when night fell.) Among the navigational aids developed at McCook was the radio beacon to guide pilots along an established airway, first installed in United States airmail planes in 1925.

McCook was active in designing and building experimental aircraft until 1924, after which the field confined its activities to monitoring private industry models. Among aircraft designed or built at McCook were the first military ambulance plane, a Fokker T-2 modified under the direction of I. M. Laddon in 1923; the first military helicopter; the Barling Bomber and the Verville-Sperry Messenger.

The first military helicopter was built at McCook under contract with Russian refugee Dr. George de Bothezat. First flown on December 19, 1922 by Major Thurman H. Bane, the field's commander, and later by Lieutenant Harris, the helicopter proved a disappointment. The machine was hard to pilot and while it could fly straight up, it could not fly forward. De Bothezat's contract was terminated in 1924.

The Barling Bomber, a six engine triplane, was the largest airplane of its day. First tested in August 1923 by McCook pilots Lieutenants Harold R. Harris and Muir S. Fairchild, this machine also proved a disappointment. Although it set several weight-carrying records with loads up to 6,600 pounds, it could not safely clear the Appalachian Mountains. The Barling was built under a competitive contract won by Witteman-Lewis in Teterboro, New Jersey. One story has it that the Barling was destroyed some years later in a mysteriously-predicted hangar fire at Wilbur Wright Field (see EA 4).

The Verville-Sperry Messenger, the smallest airplane of its day, proved a success. It was developed at McCook under the direction of Alfred V. Verville in 1919-1920 to serve as an Army courier plane, hence the name Messenger. A racing version, the Verville-Sperry R-2, piloted by Lieutenant H. H. Miller, won the Pulitzer Trophy during the International Air Races at Wilbur Wright Field on October 2-4, 1924, with a speed of 216.72 miles per hour. A military version, the Verville-Sperry M-1, took part in the first docking of an airplane and an airship, on September 18, 1923 over Langley Field, Virginia. In the exercise, the Messenger flew under a D-3 airship to land on a hanging trapeze. A Verville-Sperry M-1 is on display at the United States Air Force Museum (EA 1).

McCook developed numerous improvements to the airplane propeller and the airplane engine. Propeller improvements included controllable-pitch and reverse-pitch, and engine improvements, the supercharger and the air-cooled radial engine.

Among the many civilian applications developed at McCook was the first use of an airplane for crop-dusting. In a 1921 pioneer flight, Lieutenant Macready piloted a Curtiss JN-6 while Etienne Dormoy sprayed insecticide over a large grove of catalpa trees that were suffering from "catalpa sphinx." The experiment was requested by the United States Department of Agriculture.

After the end of World War I, the major overall mission of McCook Field was to support the development of the United States aircraft industry. As a result of this cooperative program between military and civilian aviation, many of the industry's leaders made extended visits to the field. Among them were Glenn Curtiss, Chance Vought, William Boeing, Allan Lockheed and Donald Douglas, as well as Lawrence Sperry, Sr. (see CL 6) and Grover Loening (see SL 6). In connection with this mission, McCook established an aviation information clearinghouse for use by manufacturers, students and others, which circulated 12,490 documents in 1924 alone.

In 1927 McCook's activities were moved to the new Wright Field, now part of Wright-Patterson Air Force Base (EA 4), where many of McCook's original lines of investigation are still being pursued today.

McCook Field was named for General Alexander McDowell McCook, who once owned part of the land on which it was built. The General was a member of a family known as "the Fighting McCooks" because of their military service to the Union during the Civil War.

His wife, Kate Phillips, was the daughter of Jonathan D. Phillips, the original owner of the Grey Manor, which once stood at the corner of First and Ludlow Streets in Dayton. The Grey Manor, now replaced by the Talbott Tower, at one time housed offices of the Dayton Wright Airplane Company (SL 5).

The government leased the 200-acre field for $12,800 per year from the Dayton Metal Products Company, owned by Charles F. Kettering (see SL 4) and Edward A. Deeds (see SL 3). Known as North Field, the land had been partially cleared by Kettering and Deeds in anticipation of opening a flying school.

Authorized as a temporary field on October 18, 1917, McCook Field was established to centralize the widely scattered United States military aviation research activities in order to provide better support following the nation's entrance into World War I the previous April 6. The first personnel arrived in early December, less than two months after authorization. By 1919 the field had been enlarged to 254 acres with 69 buildings and a 100 by 1,340-foot runway. McCook's motto became, "This field is small. Use it all.", partly because the prevailing winds dictated that the runway be laid across the short dimension of the land.

When the need for larger quarters became apparent in the early 1920s, a group of prominent Dayton citizens formed the Dayton Air Service Committee to insure that McCook's research and development activities remained in the area. Under the leadership of Frederick B. Patterson, son of John H. Patterson, founder of the National Cash Register Company, the committee raised more than $400,000, most of which was used to buy a tract of land for a new field east of Dayton. The land was deeded to the federal government in August 1924 for a token fee of $2. Named Wright Field in honor of Wilbur and Orville Wright, the new field was dedicated October 12, 1927.

The McCook Field site is now occupied by the Kettering Athletic Field, the Parkside Homes housing project (opened in 1941), the McCook Shopping Center and other buildings.

A two-sided commemorative plaque erected in 1967 along North Bend Boulevard stands near a former entrance to McCook Field.

Photograph of McCook Field taken by pioneer aerial photographer Lieutenant George Goddard on July 4, 1926. The picture was taken by flashlight at 10:30 p.m. while flying at 1,000 feet. The white crosses point toward frequent destinations, such as Chicago.

NL 2 First Emergency Freefall Parachute Jump Landing Site
335 Troy Street
Dayton, Ohio 45405

The first emergency freefall parachute jump ended in a grape arbor in the backyard of the still-standing house at 335 Troy Street. The jump was made by McCook Field (NL 1) test pilot Lieutenant Harold R. Harris on October 20, 1922. Harris' airplane crashed three blocks away in the yard of a double house that once stood at 403 Valley Street.

On the day he became the first to save his life with a modern parachute, Harris was flying a Loening Monoplane P-233 to gather data on a new aileron. His troubles began while he was engaged in mock combat with fellow test pilot Lieutenant Muir S. Fairchild, who was flying a Thomas Morse MB-2 P-259. At about 2,500 feet, Harris' plane suddenly began to vibrate so violently that he lost control and was forced to bail out to save his life.

Harris described his experience in the official report he filed the next day. He reported the control stick was "violently oscillating laterally" and that "particles of wing or aileron (were) flying from the left wing" when he decided he had no choice but to jump. However, after climbing out the top of the fuselage, where he was swept clear of the airplane by a high wind, Harris made an almost fatal mistake. As he plunged toward the earth, he began pulling on what he thought was the release ring of his parachute but was actually the leg strap of his harness. Discovering his mistake after three futile tugs, he quickly pulled the proper ring and the parachute opened with a violent jerk a few feet above the ground, giving him just enough time to pull up his legs to act as a spring, as he had been taught, before landing in the grape arbor.

Harris reported he felt no feeling of relief when the parachute finally opened, saying it was "simply part of the whole operation." To his rescuers he said, "I'm not hurt, just excited."

After leaving the Army Air Service in 1925, Harris helped form a commercial crop dusting company, then served as an executive for Peruvian Airlines, Pan American-Grace Airways (PANAGRA), American Overseas Airlines, Pan American World Airways and Northwest Airlines. He returned to the Service during World War II as chief of staff for the Air Transport Command, reaching the rank of brigadier general.

Although the new parachute, developed at McCook Field following World War I, was first successfully tested by Leslie Irvin on April 28, 1919, wearing a parachute did not become mandatory for Army airmen until January 15, 1923, five months after Harris' jump proved the value of the device.

The impetus for the development of the new parachute came out of the experience of World War I, in which many American pilots lost their lives because they were provided no means of escape from their damaged airplanes. While static-lined parachutes (carried in the airplane but not attached to the airman) were available, prevailing attitudes discouraged their use. Among pilots, using a parachute was considered an act of cowardice, while commanders feared the loss of valuable airplanes if pilots were able to bail out at the first sign of trouble. In addition, the early parachutes were highly unreliable.

The use of parachutes dates back to the days of the early balloonists when a Frenchman, who thought he was falling to his death after his hot air balloon burst, suddenly found the torn fabric changing into a parachute, wafting him magically to a safe landing. By the end of World War I, state of the art parachute design was typified by the attached-type automatic Guardian Angel, a bulky apparatus stored in the plane's fuselage, which frequently became entangled in the machine when the user attempted to jump.

The McCook Field Parachute Section, under the direction of Major E. L. Hoffman, approached the problem of developing a safe, practical parachute by first testing all available models. Finding each lacking in some respect, McCook personnel designed a new type to be operated by the user. Attached to the airman rather than tethered to the plane, this new parachute was carried first in a backpack, then in a less restricting seatpack. The first model, designated Model A, had a 40-gore straight cut Habutai silk canopy and 40 braided silk shroud

The wreck of Lieutenant Harold R. Harris' Loening Monoplane, October 20, 1922. Harris parachuted out and landed unhurt in a grape arbor a few blocks away on Troy Street, the first to save his life with a freefall parachute.

lines. Today's modern parachutes are still based on principles developed at McCook Field.

Later, at Wright Field (see EA 4), Hoffman developed the two-parachute system used on America's space capsules. James M. Russell, one of his assistants, developed the Russell-Lobe parachute

after leaving the Army in 1924. Leslie Irvin, the first person to test the new parachute, left McCook shortly afterwards to form the Irving Air Chute Company in Buffalo, New York. (The "g" was inadvertently added when filing for incorporation and never removed.)

Harris' 1922 jump led to the formation of the Caterpillar

Club, named for the worm that produced the silk from which early parachutes were made. The idea for the club came from Milton St. Clair, a McCook parachute engineer, and two *Dayton Evening Herald* newsmen: Maurice Hutton, the paper's aviation editor, and Verne Timmerman, a photographer. Timmerman suggested forming a bail out club after viewing souvenirs of the Harris jump. A few days later St. Clair came up with the name and Irvin agreed to give a gold caterpillar pin with ruby eyes to each person who qualified. The club had no meetings, no officers and no dues.

Membership in the Caterpillar Club was open to any person whose life was saved by a freefall parachute after jumping from a disabled airplane. Although Harris technically was the first to qualify, the roster was back-dated in 1929 to add three others not actually meeting the official criteria, including two who jumped from the blimp *Wingfoot Express* when it burst into flames over Chicago on July 21, 1919 (see NL 10).

By the end of 1929 membership in the Caterpillar Club reached 202. At that time the member with the largest number of emergency jumps was Charles A. Lindbergh, who survived four: two while in the Air Corps in 1925 and two while an airmail pilot in 1926. By 1955 the club's roster had grown to more than 40,500.

335 Troy Street is a private residence and not open to the public.

NL 3   Former McGuire Products Company Factory
206 Troy Street
Dayton, Ohio 45404

The building at 206 Troy Street was once the workshop of Roy McGuire, inventor of early aviation instruments, including the Little Robot automatic pilot.

Developed in the 1930s specifically for use on light airplanes, for which the heavy, costly earlier automatic pilots were impractical, the Little Robot was one of McGuire's most important inventions. Weighing less than five pounds and selling for a relatively inexpensive $300, the Little Robot kept the airplane on course and automatically corrected for a spin. This overcame a hazard that had cost many lives: the inability of a pilot to tell when a plane was in a spin during hazy weather until the machine dropped through the overcast, by which time it was usually too late to prevent a crash.

The Little Robot was the first to use a tilted rate gyro, on which McGuire held the original patent, a principle still employed in many of the automatic pilots produced today. Based on a conventional bank and turn indicator, the Little Robot was mounted on the control panel at a 35-degree angle, enabling it to make corrections on two axes, lateral and directional, while a conventionally-mounted instrument was capable of directional control only.

The Little Robot was activated by a variation in the turn indicator which initiated a vacuum supply (from either a venturi or a pump) to a piston connected to a tab on the rudder, thus correcting for any deviation from the set course. The course was automatically determined by a radio compass tuned to a radio station at the destination.

During World War II McGuire adapted his automatic pilot for use on glide bombs, manufacturing several thousand of the instruments. However, none were used in the war, possibly because they turned out to be too large or too heavy for their intended function. Interested in photography as well as aviation, McGuire also developed the first aerial polaroid camera.

McGuire took up aviation at an early age. He learned to fly in a JN4D, made his first solo flight on his 16th birthday, October 13, 1922, and was granted his pilot's license in 1929. He logged over 30,000 hours in his half-century of flying as a barnstormer, for the movies, as a test pilot, as a commercial airline pilot and in his own planes, a Monocoupe and later a 1959 Comanche.

McGuire first came to Dayton in 1939 as manager of the southern and western division of Lear Avia, Inc. (NL 10), manufacturer of the Learscope and other aviation instruments. In 1941 he formed his own company, Instrument Design, Inc., to manufacture aircraft instruments. The company moved to 206 Troy Street in 1946.

Four years later the name was changed to McGuire Products Company.

In 1976 McGuire and Clayton J. Brukner, co-founder of the Waco Aircraft Company (NL 5), were honored by having local aviation radio facilities named for them. The Montgomery County omni-range at Dayton-Wright Brothers Airport on Springboro Pike, is now the McGuire VOR. The Gem City radio beacon located six miles southwest of Dayton International Airport (NL 11) was renamed the Brukner beacon. The Brukner beacon has since been replaced by newer technology.

The first radio beacon system of aerial navigation, origin of the expression "flying on the beam," was developed at McCook Field (NL 1). The very high frequency omni-range (VOR) system, adopted in 1957, uses a VHF radio signal. The non-directional beam, developed previous to the VOR method, transmits on medium frequency (MF), sending a continuous tone in all directions, interrupted at 30-second intervals with identifying Morse code letters.

Roy McGuire died March 6, 1980 at the age of 73. Upon his death, the company was inherited by a longtime employee. It has now gone out of business and the building is occupied by another enterprise.

NL 4   Former International Flare and Signal Company Office
The American Legion Post 586
North Third Street and Park Avenue
Tipp City, Ohio 45371

The American Legion Hall was once the office building for the International Flare and Signal Company, developer of the first electronically-controlled airplane flare, the Driggs-Faber system.

Developed at the beginning of World War II, the Driggs-

Faber system provided a longer period of illumination than was possible with the previous pistol-type flares. The system was designed to address the need of the larger aircraft being produced for the war, which required more time to make a safe landing in an emergency. Mounted on the side of an airplane, the flare was electronically controlled by a switch in the cockpit. Upon release, the flare floated to earth suspended from a parachute to slow its descent, lighting up the ground for one, one and one-half or three minutes depending on its size. The Driggs-Faber system was used by American and British airplanes during World War II and is still used today by small commercial aircraft.

International Flare manufactured several other products used in World War II, including cartridges for starting the engines of airplanes on United States aircraft carriers. Among the company's experimental work towards the end of the war was development of a pressed powder rocket candle, forerunner of today's space rockets.

Before developing the Driggs-Faber system, one of International Flare's main products was a pistol-type marine flare, used by ships as a distress signal or for identification. Made in several colors, the marine flares could be set off in a series: for example, a Coast Guard ship was identified by the series red-white-red.

International Flare dates back to 1921 when the Tipp Fireworks Company was formed by J. A. Scheip, J. R. Scheip and Carl Moser. Moser, who bought out the Scheips in 1927, was known throughout the United States as a designer of major fireworks displays. He boasted that no one was ever killed at one of his exhibitions because he exercised every precaution -- and carried $100,000 worth of insurance.

Several years after Moser acquired the company, Tipp Fireworks merged with the Kilgore Manufacturing Company of Westerville, Ohio. Renamed the International Flare and Signal Company, the business continued as a subsidiary of Kilgore until the late 1940s when the operation was moved to Westerville. A second Kilgore subsidiary, the Pullmatch Company, also was located in Tipp City during the 1940s.

To accommodate its expanded business during World War II,

International Flare erected over 300 small buildings, the largest 20 by 40 feet, in a field east of the railroad tracks behind its office building on Third Street. (The use of many small buildings, rather than one larger one, was a safety measure to minimize the risk of a fire or explosion in one area spreading to the rest of the operation.) After the war, the buildings were acquired by a lumber company, which sold them to individuals for housing, farm buildings and other uses. Remnants of some of the original foundations still remain, hidden in the undergrowth in the field between North Fifth Street and the railroad tracks on both sides of Park Street.

International Flare also occupied ten buildings on Fourth Street. Some of the later buildings, between Kilgore Boulevard and North Street, are now occupied by part of the A. O. Smith Company complex.

The American Legion is a private club and not open to the public.

NL 5   Former Waco Aircraft Company Factory
B. F. Goodrich Aerospace
Waco Street
Troy, Ohio 45373

The Waco Aircraft Company, a leading airplane manufacturer in the period between World War I and World War II, once occupied part of the B. F. Goodrich plant in Troy's Archer Industrial Park. Waco airplanes included models designed for racing and exhibition, for commercial uses, for use as private airplanes, for the export market, and for governmental and military use.

Organized in 1923 by Clayton J. Brukner and Elwood "Sam" Junkin, the company initially promoted its products by exhibiting its airplanes at national aviation events and entering them in competitions. Early models included the Model Seven and Model Eight, which were displayed at the 1924 International Air Races held at Wilbur Wright Field (see EA 4). The Model Seven, the company's second production model, was a three-seat open cockpit biplane. The Model Eight (only one was built) was a seven-person enclosed cabin biplane.

Waco's next two models, the Model Nine and Model Ten, quickly brought national recognition to the company with their outstanding performance in major competitions. Among events won by Waco aircraft were the first annual Commercial Airplane Reliability Tour, in 1925, won by a Model Nine that finished with a perfect score; and the 1927 Transcontinental Air Races, won by a Model Ten.

The popular Model Nine was a two-seat open cockpit biplane with a 29-foot wing span, a weight of 1,090 pounds empty, a range of 400 miles, and a maximum speed of 92 miles per hour. The price was $2,500, later reduced to $2,250. The Model Ten, also a two-seat open cockpit biplane, was called "the greatest Waco ever built." The Model Ten sold for $2,385 to $2,460. With this model, introduced in 1927, production reached two airplanes per working day, with sales double that of all competitors combined.

Among commercial users of Waco aircraft were operators of airmail, delivery, and passenger airlines, including Clifford Ball and Northwest Airways, Inc. Ball purchased four Model Nines for his United States airmail service, which later evolved into Pennsylvania Central, then Capitol Airlines. Northwest Airways, Inc., of Minneapolis, Minnesota, purchased three JYM Taperwings for its airmail service to Seattle and Chicago. The JYM, produced in 1929, was an open cockpit two-seat biplane with a special cover over the front seat to protect the mail.

Representative of the many organizations that purchased Wacos for company use were Egyptian Produce Trading Company, of Alexandria, Egypt, a 1934 YKC; Buchanan Drilling Company of San Antonio, Texas, a 1936 ZQC-6; and Republic Steel Corporation, which purchased seven 1937 Cabin Wacos to carry food to the company's Warren and Niles, Ohio plants during a 26-day period of labor problems.

Waco airplanes also were popular with private owners, including many well-known people in the United States and abroad. Among

Waco Model Nine, built in 1925.

these were British aviatrix Lady Grace Hay Drummond-Hay, Howard Hughes, Phil Harris, Leland Hayward and Katharine Hepburn.

As the popularity of the Waco airplanes grew, many of the company's famous customers started coming to Troy to pick up their planes at the factory, staying at the Hotel Lollis, on the corner of West Franklin and South Market Streets, while awaiting delivery. (The hotel is now the Morris House, a senior citizens apartment building.) By 1926 the demand for Waco airplanes had grown so great that a "Waiting for Waco Club" was formed whereby delivery of a new plane was assigned in the order in which the guests registered at the hotel. As a result, as much as $900 often was offered by a late arrival to trade places with the person at the top of the list.

Waco's extensive export market covered countries throughout the world, including Norway, England, South Africa, China, Iran, India, Canada and numerous countries in Central and South America. Among the company's export activities were the sale of 1929 Taperwings to China, Mexico, Cuba and El Salvador for pursuit and training; and the development in the early 1930s of a convertible airmail plane equipped with mounts for two machine guns and racks for five small or two large bombs, which proved popular in Central and South America where political revolutions were frequent occurrences. Other exports included a 1935 Standard Cabin, named *Friend of Iran*, which was used for two years in a project to uncover ancient cities buried in the desert sands of Persia.

Governmental customers in the United States included the state of Ohio, which purchased a 1938 Model C-8 that had been used as a demonstrator, and the Coast Guard, which purchased three EQC-6 models furnished with skis as well as wheels.

As World War II approached, Waco's focus changed dramatically from production for a predominately civilian and export market to full production for the United States military, starting with a contract in 1939 to manufacture 600 modified F-7 models for the Army Air Corps Civilian Pilot Training Program (CPTP).

With the completion of the CPTP contract at the end of 1942, the company concentrated solely on the production of gliders for the war effort. Designed by Waco, which manufactured 1,607 of the total 13,402 produced (the remainder were built by sub-contractors), the gliders were used to transport troops, equipment and supplies. A 13-passenger CG4A Waco glider like those used to land troops on Normandy during the invasion of France on D-Day, June 6, 1944, is on display at the United States Air Force Museum (EA 1).

When World II ended, Waco was unsuccessful in competing in the post-war market and consequently dropped aircraft production entirely.

Over the years a number of well-known pilots were associated with Waco, including John H. Livingston and Charles A. Lindbergh. Richard Bach, a biplane enthusiast, named his book *Jonathan Livingston Seagull* after Livingston, Waco's chief test pilot and winner of many national airplane races. Lindbergh, who was the first to fly non-stop across the Atlantic, in 1927, making the flight in 33.5 hours, once ferried Waco airplanes from the factory in Troy to distributors' airfields.

Waco's roots went back to the Weaver Aircraft Company, formed in Loraine, Ohio in 1920 by Clayton J. Brukner and Elwood "Sam" Junkin, and named for George E. "Buck" Weaver, who helped negotiate the financing. The company's initials, WACO, became the name of its product, Waco airplanes, and eventually the official name of the company.

In 1921 Brukner and Junkin moved to Medina, Ohio at the invitation of Howard Calvert and his father-in-law, A. I. Root. Root was the first to publish an eye-witness account of a Wright brothers flight (see EA 3). Calvert and his wife Elvira later were killed in the crash of a Waco Model Five, one of three built in Medina.

In 1923 Brukner and Junkin moved their operation to Troy, Ohio. There they set up a factory in the vacant Pioneer Pole and Shaft Company building at 635 Union Street and changed the name of the company to Advance Aircraft Company. Financing for the new venture came from a chance meeting with 21-year-old Alden Sampson II, the beneficiary of a $6,000,000 trust fund. (Sampson had run away from his home in New York five years earlier and was then living in nearby Tipp City, Ohio.) The attorneys for Sampson's trust agreed to buy $20,000 worth of stock on the condition the company employ

A Waco glider used in World War II. The glider could carry up to 15 men.

Sampson. Brukner and Junkin later bought out Sampson's share after he lost interest in the business.

As business increased, the company opened several more plants and established a flying field, called the Park Board Field, on city-owned land along Staunton Road, where the Hobart Arena and the high school stadium now stand.

In 1928 the company consolidated its widely-scattered operations at its final location, a 120-acre field bounded by High Street, Peters Avenue and the New York Central railroad. After considering other locations, the company decided to remain in Troy when a public subscription campaign, "Keep Waco in Troy," raised $19,000 to pur-

chase the land. A year later the company's name was changed to Waco Aircraft Company to better identify with the popular name for its airplanes.

In addition to the skills of the company's designers and engineers, several elements contributed to Waco's success during the 1920s and 1930s: the early practice of requiring an advance cash deposit on each order, the ability of Waco airplanes to operate out of smaller fields than competing aircraft, and the strategy of expanding the company's export market during the depression of the 1930s.

When Waco failed to gain a place in the post-World War II aircraft market, the company diversified into other products, including the well-received Lickety Log Splitter, a mechanical wood splitter developed by Brukner. In 1946 Waco consolidated all operations at its office building and sold the factory to the B. F. Goodrich Company, then ceased operations entirely after being acquired by Allied Aero Industries of Syracuse, New York in 1963.

Brukner and Junkin first became acquainted as students at Central High School, Battle Creek, Michigan, from which the two graduated in 1915. Junkin, married in 1925 to Hattie Weaver (the widow of "Buck" Weaver, for whom the company originally was named), died of a heart condition in 1926 at the age of 29. Brukner, who never married, died in 1977 at the age of 81. At Brukner's funeral on December 29, 1977, three pilots flew the "missing man formation" in their open cockpit Wacos, led by Harold Johnson, local airport operator and exhibition flyer known as the Red Baron.

Today, two groups are active in preserving Waco's memory and a third is engaged in manufacturing replicas of the original airplane.

The National Waco Club, headquartered in Hamilton, Ohio, is dedicated to the restoration, preservation and flying of original Waco airplanes. Around 400 of these aircraft are currently in flying condition.

The Waco Historical Society, incorporated as a nonprofit corporation in 1979, is dedicated to the preservation and perpetuation of the history and artifacts of the Waco Aircraft Company. It operates the WACO Aircraft Museum in Troy, Ohio (NL 6).

Classic Aircraft, Inc., of Lansing, Michigan, manufactures replicas of the popular Waco Model YMF-5. To date, about 70 of these new Wacos have been produced, with a price tag of about $250,000 each.

The Brukner Nature Center at 5995 Horseshoe Bend Road (which runs off Route 55 about two miles west of I-75 Exit 73) was established by Brukner in 1967 on a 146-acre wildlife preserve he owned. The Center's exhibits include a display about Clayton Brukner.

B. F. Goodrich Aerospace is not open to the public.

NL 6   WACO Aircraft Museum
105 South Market Street
Troy, Ohio 45373

The WACO Aircraft Museum is operated by the Waco Historical Society, Inc. It tells the story of the Waco Aircraft Company (see SL 5), the country's largest producer of civilian aircraft in the period between the two World Wars.

The museum tells the story through photographs, scale models of some of the company's aircraft and various artifacts and memorabilia. Among the exhibits are the original framework of a Model UPF-7 airplane, a scale model of a Model PG-7 powered glider, an original Waco Cabin throw-over control column from the estate of Clayton Brukner, an OX-5 propeller manufactured by nearby Hartzell Propeller (NL 7) and numerous albums of photographs related to the company and its aircraft.

The museum also has a research library, maintains a computerized listing of Waco airplanes, manages a mobile exhibit created in cooperation with B. F. Goodrich Aerospace that travels to various aviation-related events and sponsors an annual fly-in of Waco airplanes.

The WACO Aircraft Museum is open 1:00 to 5:00 p.m. on Saturdays and Sundays from May through November, or by appointment by telephoning 937-335-9226 or 937-335-1742. Admission is free.

NL 7   Hartzell Propeller Inc.
One Propeller Place
Piqua, Ohio 45356

Hartzell Propeller Inc. is the world leader in the manufacture of propeller systems, with 85 percent of the corporate turboprop market and 60 percent of the turboprop airliner market.

Hartzell's lineage goes back to a company started in 1917, just 14 years after Wilbur and Orville Wright invented the airplane. Among the company's earliest customers were two Dayton area companies, the Dayton Wright Airplane Company (SL 5) and Waco Aircraft Company (NL 5), as well as a company started by a one-time manager of The Wright Company (WA 11), Grover Loening.

Dayton Wright airplanes equipped with Hartzell propellers included the R. B. Racer, designed to compete in the 1920 Gordon Bennett race and listed in *Jane's 100 Significant Aircraft*, and the O.W.I. Aerial Sedan, the last Dayton Wright airplane on which Orville Wright worked.

Hartzell propellers were used on many models produced by the Waco Aircraft Company, located in nearby Troy. Among these were the Model Nine (1925), on which Waco first introduced its new welded steel tube fuselage construction, and the Model F (1930), an economy model priced at $4,250 that was called "the easiest flying airplane in America."

Among Loening airplanes equipped with Hartzell propellers were three military models manufactured around 1919: a Monoplane purchased by the United States Army, a Monoplane purchased by the United States Navy for shipboard use and a Seaplane that broke the world altitude record for an airplane carrying two people.

In the early 1920s Hartzell experimented with building airplanes, including the development of the first airplane made of plywood. Hartzell models included the FC-1 and FC-2, both two-seat open cockpit biplanes. A FC-1 flown by Walter Lees, an employee of the Johnson Flying Service (see NL 11), placed first in the National Cash Register race at the 1924 International Air Races at Wilbur

Wright Field (see EA 4). Lees later was associated with the development of the first diesel aircraft engine, announced in 1930, while with the Packard automobile company.

Hartzell made history again in 1986 when it made the propellers for the *Voyager*, the first airplane to fly nonstop around the world without refueling. Hartzell joined the project almost at the last minute when it was asked to make replacement propellers after those manufactured by another company failed in a test flight at the end of September 1986. After the failure, the planners decided to abandon the wooden-type propellers, initially chosen because they weighed less, in favor of the heavier metal-type, which was deemed to be more reliable. Thus, Hartzell, a leading maker of the metal-type, was asked to make the replacements. Although inexperienced in the unique system required for the experimental aircraft, Hartzell was able to complete the new propellers within the 16 days requested, spending only about a week on the actual production process.

The *Voyager* project was first proposed by the airplane's designer, Burt Rutan. The co-pilots were his brother, Dick Rutan, and Jeana Yeager. The aircraft was made almost entirely of extremely lightweight composite materials. It had an 111-foot wingspan, weighed 1,859 pounds empty and could carry 1,200 gallons of fuel. It was equipped with two engines, one in the nose and one in the tail, and two Hartzell propellers, with the rear propeller able to reverse thrust for landing.

The record-setting flight took nine days, from December 14 to 23, to fly the 26,678-mile circuit from Edwards Air Force Base, California and return. After being on public display for a time in California, the *Voyager* was turned over to the Smithsonian Institution, never to be flown again.

Hartzell Propeller was established in 1917 as a division of the George W. Hartzell Company, a producer of walnut lumber. It was born as a result of an embargo imposed by the United States at the beginning of World War I. Cut off from its markets in England and Germany, which accounted for the company's entire output, Hartzell turned to the production of airplane propellers to offset part of the lost business. The propellers were made of walnut lumber, the company's

The Dayton Wright Airplane Company's R. B. Racer, built for the 1920 Gordon Bennett race. Note the Hartzell Walnut Propeller Company insignia on the upper propeller blade.

former product. Thus, the new venture was named Hartzell Walnut Propeller Company.

Hartzell's first prototype propellers were chopped with hatchets out of blocks of laminated walnut by the company's president, Robert N. Hartzell, assisted by the company carpenter -- the same method used by the Wright brothers when they fashioned the propel-

lers for their Flyer I. Never actually used on an airplane, the results of these first crude attempts showed that more scientific design and construction methods were needed.

Hartzell Propeller's initial products were fixed pitch propellers, mainly made of wood, with a few made of duraluminium. In the following years Hartzell became a pioneer in selective pitch propellers, developed the world's first composite counterweight propeller incorporating the reversing (beta) system in the early 1950s and introduced a five-blade propeller to reduce noise and vibration in 1975.

The Hartzell Company dates back to 1875 when John T. Hartzell started a small circle sawmill in Greenville, Ohio. Among the company's first products was lumber for building wagons, which soon led to Hartzell's expansion into the production of farm wagons. John's son, George, joined his father in the business in 1890. Ten years later George bought out his father, moved the company to Piqua and changed the name to George W. Hartzell Company. George's son, Robert N., who entered the business in 1917 to set up the propeller division, became president of the company upon George's death in 1933.

By 1975, 100 years after its founding, Hartzell was comprised of four divisions and five companies, including the airplane propeller company. In 1981 the Hartzell family sold the Hartzell Propeller Company to TRW, Inc. while retaining control of the rest of the business. The propeller company then became the TRW Hartzell Propeller Division of TRW, Inc.

In 1987 TRW sold its propeller division, which then became the privately-owned Hartzell Propeller Inc. The propeller company is now in the process of moving its offices from the original Hartzell Propeller building at 350 Washington Avenue to its new plant at One Propeller Place.

The company currently manufactures two- to six-blade constant-speed propellers made of aluminum or composite material.

Hartzell Propeller Inc. is not open to the public.

NL 8   McCauley Accessory Division
Cessna Aircraft Company
3535 McCauley Drive
Vandalia, Ohio 45377

McCauley Accessory Division, located at the Dayton International Airport Industrial Park, is a major producer of propellers for light aircraft. Founded in 1935 by Ernest G. McCauley, a former aerodynamics engineer at McCook Field (NL 1) and Wright Field (see EA 4), the history of McCauley reflects the development of the propeller from the pre-World War II era to the present time.

A propeller works like a small wing, a principle discovered by the Wright brothers in 1903. The rotation of the propeller, mounted on a revolving powered shaft, creates horizontal thrust that propels the aircraft forward. A fixed pitch propeller presents a constant angle of attack to the air flow; a variable-pitch propeller can change the angle to generate the maximum amount of thrust for a given amount of power. The amount of power a propeller can absorb and transform into thrust is determined by the number and shape of its blades, its diameter and the speed at which it rotates. The first airplane propellers had two blades, were fixed-pitch and were whittled from wood.

By the time McCauley entered the business, propellers made of materials other than wood were starting to enter the market. McCauley was a pioneer in the use of the new materials, developing the first all-metal (steel) propeller to be sold in America and the first forged aluminum fixed-pitch propeller. Both were designed by company founder Ernest G. McCauley, who had raised the funds to start the business by selling the patent on one of his inventions, the first hydraulic counterweight propeller.

During World War II, McCauley manufactured propellers for American military aircraft. A number of the 20,000 solid steel propellers produced for the war are still in use today, mainly on agricultural aircraft. A Stearman PT-13 World War II trainer equipped with a McCauley propeller is on display at the United States Air Force Museum (EA 1).

When World War II ended McCauley turned to the personal and business aircraft market, a market in which, previous to the war, wooden propellers had been the norm. The company entered the market with a new lightweight one-piece forged aluminum fixed-pitch propeller carrying the trade-name Met-L-Prop. The Cessna Bird Dog airplane at the United States Air Force Museum is equipped with a propeller of this type.

Since then, each decade brought improved products. The Met-L-Matic, a metal constant-speed variable-pitch propeller, appeared in the 1950s. The Feth-R-Matic series, constant-speed full-feathering propellers that increased aircraft controllability by changing the angle of the blade, followed in the 1960s. Three-blade constant-speed propellers with threadless retention and three-blade turbine propellers were developed during the 1970s. In the 1980s, the company brought out four-blade turbine propellers and composite fiberglass-aluminum propellers. And in the 1990s it introduced a lightweight, low-noise five-blade aluminum model aimed at markets with especially strict noise level rules.

The company started as McCauley Aviation Corporation in a factory at 2901 West Third Street. In 1941 McCauley moved to 2900 West Second Street, then two years later to 1840 Howell Avenue (all in Dayton), where it remained for the next 35 years. McCauley has been at its present location since 1978.

After Ernest McCauley's retirement in 1950, the company operated under various ownerships until it was acquired by Cessna Aircraft Company in 1960. In 1986 Cessna was acquired by General Dynamics Corporation, which sold it to Textron, Inc. in 1992.

Cessna's roots go back to a company called Travel Air, organized by Clyde Cessna, Walter Beech and Lloyd Stearman in Wichita, Kansas in 1924. Today, Cessna Aircraft Company produces general aviation aircraft, a classification that includes all aircraft except commercial airliners and military airplanes. Interestingly, Clyde Cessna's Travel Air company was forced to close during the early years of the 1930s depression, reopening later in the decade, while one of its competitors, Waco Aircraft Company (NL 5), now defunct, was enjoying a premier position in the airplane market.

McCauley Accessory Division is not open to the public.

NL 9   Former Aeroproducts Factory
Delphi Chassis Division Vandalia Operations
General Motors Corporation
480 North Dixie Drive
Vandalia, Ohio 45377

The Delphi Chassis Vandalia plant originally was constructed as a factory for the General Motors Aeroproducts Division, established in 1940 to manufacture Aeroprop airplane propellers. Aeroproducts was absorbed by the General Motors Allison Division in 1961.

The Aeroprop, used extensively on World War II military aircraft, was a hydraulic, full-feathering, constant-speed, unit-constructed propeller with an innovative lightweight hollow ribbed steel blade and dual rotation. (Dual rotation or contra-rotation propellers were mounted one behind the other and geared to turn in opposite directions, an arrangement intended to keep the slipstream straight and eliminate torque.) The line included two-blade, three-blade, four-blade and six-blade models.

The Aeroprop incorporated many desirable features, including ease of installation and maintenance. Designed for routine installation in less than 20 minutes, one energetic crew reportedly removed an Aeroprop and replaced it with another in 12 minutes flat.

Among World War II airplanes with Aeroprop propellers was the Bell P-39 Aerocobra, a first-line pursuit airplane. Of the 9,584 Aerocobras produced, 4,773 were allocated to the Soviet Union. A Bell P-39 Aerocobra is on display at the United States Air Force Museum (EA 1) along with an exhibit about the Aeroprop propeller.

Aeroproducts was an outstanding example of the rapid response of American industry to the demands of the military during World War II. Soon after the division was formed in June 1940, Aeroproducts found that the product it had planned to perfect over a six-year period was needed immediately to fight the war, which had started in Europe in 1939. Aeroproducts responded to the emergency by speeding up construction and development plans. In March 1941, nine months after it was established and five months after breaking ground, the division moved into its new factory. By December 7, 1941, the day the Japanese attacked Pearl Harbor, Hawaii, the plant was in its first month of full production.

After America entered the war, Aeroprop production increased dramatically, rising from a total of 730 units in December 1941 to well over 10,000 units per month two years later. One factor contributing to this rapid increase in production was the vast reduction in the amount of time required to grind a blade. The initial grinding time of 20 hours per blade fell to just six and one-half hours 18 months later as new machinery was refined and workers acquired experience.

Much of the Aeroproducts machinery was made specifically to produce the Aeroprop, a new design for which there were few machining precedents. Among the many improvements dictated by experience was a switch from a machine set-up that accommodated only one type of production to a set-up with interchangeable tools to accommodate several models; for example, a three- or four-way hub machine.

In addition to new untried machinery, Aeroproducts faced the problem of training workers -- farmers, salesmen, housewives and others, drawn mainly from a ten-county area north of the National Highway (Route 40). Ninety-nine percent of the division's 2,500 employees had never worked on a propeller and many were untrained in any type of factory work. Nevertheless, before the war ended workers were winning government "E" awards for "Meritorious services on the production front."

The Aeroprop was developed by W. J. Blanchard and Charles J. MacNeil, founders of Engineering Products, Inc. Established in 1935, Engineering Products developed experimental propellers but had no production facilities. In 1940 the company was acquired by General Motors (GM), which viewed the acquisition as an opportunity to apply its vast production experience to the aircraft industry. Subsequently, Aeroproducts was formed and Blanchard became general manager of the new GM division.

Following the end of World War II, Aeroproducts produced propellers for peacetime use and for the Korean War (1950-1953), as well as parts for other GM divisions. In 1961 Aeroproducts' activities were transferred to the GM Allison Division in Indianapolis, Indiana and the Vandalia plant was closed.

Several years after Aeroproducts moved out, the GM Inland Division acquired the vacant plant to provide room for expansion. Inland was started in two buildings originally constructed for The Wright Company (see WA 11). In 1989 Inland was merged into the Delco Products Division, which then evolved into the Delphi Chassis Division.

The Delphi Chassis Vandalia plant is not open to the public.

NL 10   Former Lear Avia, Inc. Factory
437 North Dixie Drive
Vandalia, Ohio 45377

Lear Avia, Inc., a radio and airplane instruments company owned by William P. Lear, occupied the building at 437 North Dixie Drive from 1936 to 1941. Lear later became known as the developer of the Learjet, the world's first executive jet airplane.

Among the products produced at the Lear Vandalia factory were aircraft navigation instruments, which evolved from Lear's love of flying coupled with his vast experience in radio. Lear's interest in flying dated back to a flying exhibition he attended as a youth in Dubuque, Iowa, put on by barnstormer Lincoln Beachey. Later, Lear's interest in flying became so intense that he quit his job as a Multigraph operator to work as a grease monkey at Grant Park on Chicago's lakefront in return for free airplane rides. Eventually Lear became a pilot and the owner of a series of aircraft.

Lear's radio experience dated back to his enlistment in the United States Navy, where he attended radio school toward the end of World War I. Before coming to Dayton, Lear had been responsible for several major radio inventions, including a speaker, a car radio and a tuner. The speaker evolved into the Majestic radio. The car radio led to the establishment of the Motorola Company ("motor" for car and "ola" for Victrola, at that time the popular name for a phonograph). The tuner became the Radio Corporation of America's (RCA) "magic brain," a semiautomatic tuning mechanism. The substantial proceeds from the RCA tuner provided the funds for Lear to form his own company in l934 to manufacture aircraft radios and instruments.

One of the aviation navigation instruments manufactured at the Vandalia plant was the first commercial radio compass for airplanes, invented by Lear. Called the Learscope, the radio compass enabled the pilot to navigate by following a dot-dash signal broadcast by the Department of Commerce.

The increased demand for Lear Avia's products that came after America became a participant in World War II at the end of 1941 forced the company to move to larger quarters in a building at the corner of Young and Weber Streets in nearby Piqua. There the factory worked around the clock to keep up with the demand for aircraft radios, direction finders and other aviation instruments. Among the World War II aircraft equipped with Lear products were the B-24 and B-29.

Lear's inventions during his Dayton-Piqua period included the Learmatic Navigator, an automatic version of his Learscope radio compass, and a 24-pound automatic pilot called the C-2, the first in a series of Lear automatic pilots. A 36-pound model that made flying safe in any kind of weather earned Lear the 1950 Collier Trophy.

In 1944 Lear changed the name of his company to Lear, Inc., moved the headquarters to Grand Rapids, Michigan in 1945 and phased out the Piqua operation in 1946.

Toward the end of the 1950s, when the only civilian jet airplanes were commercial airliners, Lear began dreaming of developing a jet airplane for businessmen. Finding no support for his idea from Lear, Inc.'s board of directors, Lear sold his interest in the company to the Seigler Corporation for $14,300,000 to raise the funds to pursue his dream. The former Lear, Inc. became the Instruments Division of the merged organization, Lear-Seigler Corporation.

Lear built a factory in Wichita, Kansas and in 1963 produced the Learjet, the first executive jet airplane. In the course of developing his revolutionary plane Lear learned to fly a jet at Wright-Patterson Air Force Base (EA 4) so he could test his new airplane's automatic pilot himself.

Although the new Learjet sold well, cash flow problems forced Lear to sell his company to Gates Rubber Company in 1967 for $28,500,000. After that, Lear attempted several other projects, including building an automobile powered by steam and a turbo-prop pusher airplane called the Lear Fan, but none reached the success of his Learjet.

Except for an intervention of fate, Lear probably would have met an early death, depriving the world of his many inventions. As noted earlier, Lear once worked as a grease monkey in return for free aircraft rides at Chicago's Grant Park, then a key stop in a growing network of airmail routes. One of those rides was to have been on the blimp *Wingfoot Express* on July 21, 1919 on the blimp's third flight of the day. However, before the ropes were released, Lear was forced to give up his seat to Milton G. Norton, a Chicago news photographer. Forty-five minutes later tragedy struck while the *Wingfoot Express* floated lazily over downtown Chicago. The blimp suddenly burst into flames and crashed into the Illinois Trust and Savings Bank Building at the corner of LaSalle Street and Jackson Boulevard in the city's Loop. Ten of the bank's employees were killed as well as three of the five men in the blimp: Earl Davenport, publicity man for the White City Amusement Park where the blimp was based; mechanic Carl "Buck" Weaver; and Norton, who had taken Lear's place. The two who survived, pilot John A. Boettner and mechanic Henry Wacker, were made members number one and two of the Caterpillar Club (see NL 2).

Lear died in 1978 at the age of 75, leaving his wife of 36 years, Moya Olsen Lear. The daughter of Ole Olsen of the comedy team of Olsen and Johnson, whose shows included the 1938 Broadway hit *Hellzapoppin*, Moya had come to Piqua as a bride in 1942.

William P. Lear, Sr. (1902-1978) was inducted into the National Aviation Hall of Fame (see EA 1) in 1978.

The one-story brick building at 437 North Dixie is the only still-standing building of the three originally constructed in 1928 for the Johnson Flying Service, Inc., operator of a privately-owned airport that preceded the Dayton International Airport (NL 11), the present owner of the property.

After Lear moved his factory to Piqua, the building was occupied by the Russ Moore Flying Service, which used World War II surplus airplanes, then for a time in the 1960s by Dayton Helicopter, whose activities included flight tests for the Flight Dynamics Laboratory at Wright-Patterson Air Force Base. The last occupant was Empire Tool, a tool and die business.

The now vacant building is used for storage and is not open to the public.

NL 11   Dayton International Airport
Vandalia, Ohio 43577

The Dayton International Airport is among the top ten air cargo hubs in the United States and the site of the annual United States Air and Trade Show, which maintains permanent offices and facilities at the airport.

Established in 1975, the United States Air and Trade Show is the latest in a series of local air shows dating back to 1910, when the September 19-24 Dayton Industrial Exposition and Fall Festival featured an Aviation Day with "Aeroplane flights" by the Wright brothers at Huffman Prairie (EA 3) and other aviation events.

Other early air shows included the 1923 Labor Day air show at McCook Field (NL 1), which attracted a crowd of 100,000, and the 1924 International Air Races held October 3-5 at Wilbur Wright Field (see EA 4). The 1924 races included the bombing of a miniature New York City as the grand finale. Later, Wright Field and then Wright-Patterson Air Force Base (EA 4) sponsored various aviation shows

Aerial view of the Johnson Flying Field, located on North Dixie Drive in Vandalia from 1928 to 1936. The brick building facing Dixie is still standing in what is now General Aviation Center #2 at the Dayton International Airport.

until the early 1970s, when local community leaders and the military got together to organize the present annual event.

In 1982 the air show was expanded to include a trade show geared toward the aviation industry on the two days immediately preceding the two-day public show. Currently, the public show is an annual event; the trade show is an every two-year event held on odd-numbered years. The public show features military and civilian aircraft displays plus top-flight military and civilian flying exhibitions.

Dayton International Airport is owned and operated by the city of Dayton for the benefit of the entire region rather than by a port authority, a combination of several governmental units, as is usual with airports of this size. The city also operates Dayton-Wright Brothers Airport on Springboro Pike in Miami Township.

The Dayton airport dates back to a field established in 1928 by a group of Dayton businessmen, led by engineer and contractor Frank Hill Smith, who were convinced that in the future an airport would be as important to a city as a railroad. Located on the west side of the Dixie Highway just north of the National Road in Vandalia, the 310-acre airport was developed at a cost of $200,000, including $82,000 for the land. The facility contained three takeoff strips, a water tower, central heating plant, parking lot, two 80 by 100-foot brick and steel hangars and a one-story brick building used as a repair shop. One of the original structures, the one-story brick building, is still standing in what is now General Aviation Center #2 of Dayton International Airport. The brick building later housed the Lear Avia factory (NL 10) operated by William P. Lear, developer of the Learjet.

The airport was operated by the Johnson Flying Service, Inc. under a $9,000 per year lease with Dayton Airport, Inc., the private corporation formed by the airport's founders. E. A. "Al" Johnson, president of Johnson Flying Service, had helped the organizers select the site. In addition to operating the airport, Johnson moved his flying school and a repair shop to the new field. The repair shop had been on the southwest corner of Ludlow and Baynard Streets in Dayton and the flying school at 1507 Wilmington Pike.

The former Johnson flying school site on Wilmington was taken over by the United States military in 1944. Opened as an Army Signal Corps storage facility, the field was renamed Gentile Air Force Depot in 1951 in honor of Major Don (Dominic) S. Gentile, a World War II flying ace from Piqua, Ohio. Today, the facility is commonly identified as DESC, which stands for the Defense Electronics Supply Center, its last main tenant. In 1993 DESC was placed on a list of military bases to be closed. The city of Kettering, in which it is located, is now spearheading redevelopment of the vacated 135-acre property.

Before moving to the airport, Johnson had experimented with manufacturing airplanes, producing the Driggs-Johnson in 1924 to 1926 and the Johnson Twin 60 in 1926.

The Driggs-Johnson, an ultra light monoplane, was designed by Ivan Driggs, who soon left Johnson to form his own company. A Driggs-Johnson piloted by J. M. "Jimmy" Johnson took first place in the *Dayton Daily News* Light Airplane race at the 1924 International Air Races at Wilbur Wright Field.

The Johnson Twin 60, a two-seat open cockpit biplane, was designed by Dave E. Dunlop, who later joined Douglas Aircraft. One of the most unusual light airplanes of its period, the Twin 60 had a hull-shaped fuselage with a steel tubing frame, balanced twin rudders, a gravity feed fuel tank and a reverse pitch propeller. The machine was powered by two British Cherubs, 30 to 36 horsepower two-cylinder opposed-type air cooled engines that were mounted backwards or pusher fashion. After the Twin 60, Johnson gave up manufacturing to concentrate on airplane repairs.

In 1936, when most of the original owners had dropped out and the airport was on the verge of folding, the city of Dayton acquired ownership of the Vandalia facility in a move to qualify the airport for a Works Progress Administration (WPA) grant. The WPA was a depression era federal program designed to provide jobs for the unemployed through the funding of public works, a program for which only a publicly-owned facility could qualify. To accomplish the change from private to public ownership, a committee of local citizens under the leadership of James M. Cox raised $65,000, which was given to the city of Dayton to purchase the airport from the private owners, thus qualifying the airport for a $673,000 WPA grant to upgrade the facility. The new municipal airport was dedicated on December 17, 1936.

In 1952 the Dayton airport was named the James M. Cox Municipal Airport in honor of Cox's role in the 1936 fund-raising campaign. Cox, a Dayton newspaper publisher and a former governor of Ohio, ran as the Democratic nominee for president in 1920 with Franklin D. Roosevelt as his vice presidential running mate.

The airport was the beneficiary of another major upgrading as a result of World War II, when a Civilian Pilot Training Program

(CPTP) was established at the field and the Army Air Force used the airport to relieve the congestion at Wright Field and Patterson Field. To accommodate these new activities, the federal government increased the field by 564 acres, added a 5,500-foot runway, built eight hangars, installed fire protection and central heating systems, provided a water reservoir for emergency use and added a spur line of the Baltimore and Ohio railroad. All of these improvements accrued to the city after the war ended for a token payment of $1.

By 1946 the Dayton airport, acquired for $65,000 just ten years earlier, was worth a total of $10,000,000. The World War II Army Air Force hangar complex, reached by what is now the entrance to General Aviation Area #1, served for a time after the war as the airport's commercial aircraft center and passenger terminal. All the World War II buildings have since been demolished.

Among other landmarks in the airport's history were the construction of a new terminal building and an entrance off the National Highway (Route 40), voted upon in 1941, on the eve of World War II, but not completed until 1961; the first jet service, inaugurated in 1960; designation as an international airport in 1975; and the completion of a major terminal expansion and renovation in 1989. Today, the airport covers over 5,000 acres encompassing a total of four and one-half miles of runway, serves 17 passenger airlines, is the location of a major regional air cargo hub and is the headquarters of the only airline (PSA Airlines, Inc.) headquartered in Ohio.

Dayton International Airport is becoming an increasingly important air cargo hub, a pattern of routing that has become popular since deregulation of the airlines in 1979. In the hub system a number of an airline's flights originate out of one center, or hub, which acts as a transfer point to various other destinations. Dayton airport's status as a leading air cargo hub dates back to the opening of Emery World-wide Air Freight's Mid-American hub in November 1981. Today, Emery dispatches more than 70 airplane loads of cargo each day from the Dayton airport, with other cargo operations bringing the total up to well over 100.

A major factor in the airport's emerging prominence as an air cargo hub is its strategic location at the original "Crossroads of Amer- ica," the intersection of the historically important north-south Dixie Highway and the east-west National Road. This location places the airport in the center of the nation's top "90 Minute Market;" that is, within 90 minutes by jet airplane of over 55 percent of the country's population and businesses. Today, the modern crossroads of America lies a few miles south of the original at the intersection of north-south I-75 and east-west I-70. The original Dixie Highway is now State Route 25-A north of Vandalia, changing to Dixie Drive in Vandalia and on south. The original National Road is now U. S. Route 40.

Located adjacent to the Dayton airport to the south, and preceding it by four years, is the Amateur Trapshooting Association headquarters, host since 1924 of the Grand American Trapshooting Tournament. Darke County native Annie Oakley, "Little Miss Sureshot" of Wild West shows, was an entrant in the 1925 tournament, a year before she died in nearby Greenville, Ohio.

A two-part display about Dayton's aviation heritage is located in the lobby of the airport's terminal. The first display is a representation of the world's first man-carrying, powered, controllable flight, made by Daytonian Orville Wright on December 17, 1903 at Kitty Hawk, North Carolina. The focal point of the display is an exact 1/8-scale model of the airplane that made the first flight, from the collection of Eugene W. Kettering (see EA 1). An adjacent walk-through exhibit features a series of chronologically arranged panels that tell the story of Wilbur and Orville Wright, inventors of the airplane, and describe various other aviation-related landmark events.

Brookville Community Museum
Samuel Spitler House
14 Market Street
Brookville, Ohio 45309

The Brookville Community Museum, housed in the restored Samuel Spitler House, is a local history museum for the village of Brookville. The museum's exhibits include a display about Brookville native Warren Rasor, in his day one of the top five balloonists in the United States.

The Warren Rasor display includes notebooks, newspaper clippings, photographs, posters, logs recording the details of Rasor's balloon flights and a three-foot square wicker balloon basket, one of three remaining from the total of seven once owned by Rasor. Another of the baskets is on display at the Neil Armstrong Air and Space Museum in Wapakoneta, Ohio.

Rasor took up ballooning in 1909 at the age of 50 after his interest was aroused by watching the takeoff of the balloon *Hoosier* on the trip during which *The Dayton Journal* published the first newspaper printed in the sky (see CL 5). During his 15 years as a balloonist, Rasor made almost 100 flights, participated in many national balloon races and served as a balloon instructor in World War I. Rasor's son Herbert acted as his father's aide on many of the flights.

Rasor's first balloon trip, in 1909, was a three-hour-and-20-minute flight from Brookville to Piqua, Ohio, about 20 miles away. Rasor's longest balloon trip was from St. Louis, Missouri to Parry Sound, Ontario, Canada, a distance of 750 miles, which he covered in just under 18 hours during the 1919 National Balloon Race. Rasor took fourth place in the 1919 race, choosing to descend sooner than might have been necessary because he said at his age he did not care to take a chance of a long struggle through the wilds as might have happened had he continued farther over the barren regions of Canada. Paul J. McCullough and his aide, fellow competitors in the race who descended in the same area as Rasor, were forced to spend three days walking through the wilderness before reaching a telegraph office in

Warren Rasor's balloon *Dayton* in 1912.

Wabanik, Ontario, where they notified contest officials of their safe landing.

At the mercy of prevailing air currents, balloonists generally carried ample supplies for any emergency in addition to equipment and provisions for the trip itself. Emergency supplies often included shotguns, fishing tackle and life preservers. Equipment for the trip included instruments such as a compass, an altimeter, a stratoscope to indicate whether the balloon was traveling up or down, and a manometer to show the gas pressure in the balloon, as well as a map of the area with vital information such as the location of highly charged electrical wires. Provisions might include thermos bottles of beverages, fruit, cheese and canned goods, with cooking vessels and a bucket of unslaked lime to heat the food. (Pouring water over the unslaked lime causes it to give off intense heat, reportedly enabling food to reach the boiling point in ten minutes.)

Rasor participated in a number of national balloon races from 1912 to 1924, with his best showing being second place in the 1917 race at Muskogee, Oklahoma. The second place showing brought Rasor an invitation to participate in the 1917 Gordon Bennett International Balloon Race in Paris, France, an invitation he declined. The top place winners of the various national elimination races represented their countries in the annual Gordon Bennett race that dominated sport ballooning from 1906 until World War II.

Competition in the national balloon races was by invitation, which was extended to all clubs affiliated with the Aero Clubs of America. Rasor participated as a member of the Dayton Aero Club, whose members included L. E. Custer and Pliney M. Crume. Custer was the father of Luzern Custer, who made two balloon ascensions from the top of the Reibold Building (CL 7). Crume and Luzern were participants in the first newspaper-published-in-the-sky balloon trip.

Over the years Rasor owned a total of seven balloons. These included the *Dayton*, his first, which cost $250 and which he flew in the 1917 Muskogee, Oklahoma race, and the 50,000 cubic foot *Ohio*, which he flew in the 1919 St. Louis race. The balloons were filled with coal gas at a cost of $40 per inflation.

In addition to the national races, Rasor participated in other

Warren Rasor and his balloon *Dayton*, July 4, 1912. Warren Rasor is in the middle of the group in his shirtsleeves, with a cap and bow tie. Herbert Rasor, who served as his father's aide, is to the right of Warren.

races and sometimes gave demonstrations as promotions for local businesses.

Rasor's reputation as a balloon racer brought him an offer from Captain Albert B. Lambert to train balloonists for World War I, even though he was 58 years old at the time. Commissioned a lieutenant after he accepted the offer in November 1917, Rasor accompanied the Missouri Aeronautical School to their winter headquarters in San Antonio, Texas. During his approximately six-month Army career, Rasor carried as many as eight students at a time on training flights out of the Texas field. Military balloons, first employed in the United States during the Civil War, were used principally for observation.

Balloons, which provided man's first means of sustained flight, date back to November 21, 1783, when a hot air balloon invented by the Montgolfier brothers made a 25-minute manned flight over Paris, France. Less than a month later, on December 2, 1783, a balloon developed by Professor Jacques Charles made the first manned hydrogen balloon flight, also over Paris. Coal gas (sometimes called illuminating gas), available from public utility gas lines and favored by balloonists of Rasor's era, was introduced in 1821. Today, hot air, as used in the first balloon, is the preferred method with modern sport balloonists.

Rasor was the owner of a lumber company at 117-119 Sycamore Street in Brookville, opened a few years before he took up ballooning. Previous to establishing the lumber business, Rasor, a carpenter, built several houses in the village, including the Spitler House where the Brookville Community Museum is housed.

Warren Rasor died in 1938 at the age of 78 after refusing all his life to ride in an airplane because he considered airplanes to be "too dangerous."

In 1984 another Brookville native, Jack Halbeisen, set an aeronautic record when he became the first to fly an ultralight airplane, sometimes described as a motorized kite, from the east to the west coast and back with no ground support other than himself. Halbeisen, who was 70 years old at the time, made the 7,800 mile trip in a Pioneer FlightStar between July 25 and September 25.

The Spitler House, constructed in 1894, is considered the finest example of Queen Anne architecture in the state of Ohio. Spitler, a miller and plumber, had the house built for approximately $2,200, including $1,700 for materials and $500 for labor, after admiring similar houses during a trip to San Francisco, California. Among the many interesting features of the three-story frame dwelling are seven porches and the first indoor bathroom in Brookville. The Spitler House is listed on the National Register of Historic Places.

The Brookville Community Museum is open from 1:00 to 5:00 p.m. the first Saturday and Sunday of each month, except holidays. Admission is $1.50 for adults, $.25 for children 6 to 16 and under 6 free.

SOURCES

Listing order is first, sources listed under References, keyed by author's name and date, followed by sources other than those listed under References. Abbreviations used are:

DL   Dayton and Montgomery County Public Library
MCAB   Montgomery County Administration Building
MCHS   Montgomery County Historical Society
USAFM   United States Air Force Museum Research Department
WSU   Wright State University Archives

West Anchor

WA 1:   Aviation Trail, Inc. Board of Trustees minutes.

WA 2:   Faber 1893; Fisk 1980; Miller, Ivonette 1978; Renstrom 1975; Williams 1891-92 to 1926. Newspaper clippings, DL; deeds, MCAB; original examples of Wright and Wright printing jobs, WSU.

WA 3:   Drury 1909; Fisk 1980; Hallion 1978; Hobbs 1971; Renstrom 1975; Weaver 1983; Williams 1888-89 to 1895-96. Deeds, MCAB; Aviation Trail, Inc. Board of Trustees minutes.

WA 4:   Andrews 1975; Edison Institute 1938; Miller, Ivonette 1978; Renstrom 1975; Williams 1868-69 to 1892-93. Newspaper clippings, DL; deeds, MCAB; 1868 map of Dayton, Wright Library.

WA 5:   Kelly 1950; Renstrom 1975; Williams 1884-85 to 1891-92; Young and Fitzgerald 1983. Original copy of *The Midget*, DL; issues of *West Side News* and *The Evening Item*, DL; newspaper clippings, DL; deeds, MCAB.

WA 6:   Glines 1968; Hallion 1978; Harris 1970; Kelly 1950; Marcosson 1947; Renstrom 1975; Young and Fitzgerald 1983. Newspaper clippings, DL; deeds, MCAB.

WA 7:   Edison Institute 1938; Fisk 1980; Glines 1968; Hallion 1978; Kelly 1950; Renstrom 1975; Weaver 1983; Williams 1887-88 to 1916-17; Young and Fitzgerald 1983. Newspaper clippings, DL; deeds, MCAB; original copy of *Van Cleve Notes*, WSU.

WA 8:   Coombs 1972; Fisk 1980; Loeper 1982; Pursell 1980; Renstrom 1975; Williams 1893-94 to 1902-03; *Dayton Daily News* May 17, 1984.

WA 9:   Bryan 1978; Fisk 1980; Kelly 1950; Renstrom 1975; Williams 1892-93 to 1894-95. Ohio Historic Inventory, 1978 listing; newspaper ads, March 31 to May 15, 1893, DL.

WA 10:   Carillon Park 1982; Glines 1968; Hallion 1978; Loening 1968; Munson 1969; Renstrom 1975,1982; Whitehouse 1971; Williams 1909-10 to 1916-17; Young and Fitzgerald 1983; Harris 1970; Kelly 1950; Renstrom 1975. Delco Moraine Div., General Motors, "Delco Moraine Division of General Motors Corporation," mimeo, n.d.; newspaper clippings, DL; 1897 map of Dayton corrected to 1911, Speedwell Motor Car Co. advertisement, 1910 Industrial Exposition and Fall Festival program, MCHS; Wright Company catalogs, WSU; in person interview with Henry Cates, GM Delco Moraine Div., July 14, 1983.

WA 11:   Glines 1968; Hallion 1978; Loening 1968; Munson 1969; Renstrom 1975,1982; Wescott and Degen 1983; Williams 1911-12. Good, James M., *It Started with the Wheel: 1923-1973, 50th Anniversary*, Dayton, Oh.: Inland Div., General Motors, 1973; Geyer, Harvey D., "History of Inland," mimeo, 1948, MCHS; newspaper clippings, DL; in person interview with Terry Miller, GM Inland Div., July 13, 1982.

Central Loop

CL 1:   Andrews 1975; Kelly 1950; Miller, Ivonette 1978; Renstrom 1975.

CL 2:   Coombs 1972; Weaver 1983; Williams 1895-96, 1896-97. Rike, David L., *A Store and a City*, Dayton, Oh.: Rike's, 1969.

CL 3:   Kelly 1950; Miller, Ivonette 1978; Renstrom 1975; Young and Fitzgerald 1983. Colvin, Harriet and Myriam Page, *Sesquicentennial History of the First Regular Baptist Church: Dayton, Ohio*, Miamisburg, Oh.: The Miamisburg News, 1974; newspaper clippings, DL.

CL 4:   Drury 1909; Hallion 1978; Hobbs 1971; Marcosson 1947; Morgan 1951; Renstrom 1973; "Wright Engine No. 3," *The Engineer*, January 1985; The Engineers Club, "The Engineers Club of Dayton," mimeo, n.d.; newspaper clippings, DL.

CL 5:   Harris 1970; Kelly 1950. Newspaper clippings, DL; Dayton *Journal Herald*, July 16,1983.

CL 6:   Davenport 1978; Edison Institute 1938; Hallion 1978; Harris 1970; International Air Races, Inc. 1924; Maxwell Air Force Base n.d.; Renstrom 1975; Williams 1856-57, 1909-1910; Ball 1929. Lawrence Sperry, Sr. personnel file, USAFM.

CL 7:   Carillon Park 1982; Casey 1964; Edison Institute 1938; Solberg 1979. Typed copy of Custer's original notes of his May 2, 1923 balloon flight, Mrs. Luzern Custer.

South Loop

SL 1:   Gibbs-Smith 1971; Glines 1986; Hallion 1978; Munson 1969; Renstrom 1975; Taylor and Monday 1983; Wescott and Degen 1983. Loening quote from unpublished manuscript by Fred Marshall, private collection.

SL 2:   Crowthers 1923; Ronald and Ronald 1983; Solberg 1979; Williams 1923 to 1925. Dayton newspapers, DL; Macready personnel file, USAFM.

SL 3:   Boyd 1957; Foerste 1915; Hutchinson 1943; Leslie 1983; Marcosson 1947; Renstrom 1975. Winn, R. E., *Moraine Farm*, Dayton, Oh.: NCR, n.d.; newspaper clippings, DL.

SL 4:   Boyd 1957; Leslie 1983; Marcosson 1947; Ronald and Ronald 1983; Young 1961.

SL 5:   Angelucci 1973; Boyd 1957; Conover 1932; General Motors 1960; Hutchinson 1943; Leslie 1983; Loening 1968; Renstrom 1975; Roberts 1978; Ronald and Ronald 1983; Rolfe 1969; Smith 1939; Tavender 1967; Taylor 1969; Wagner 1982. Ventolo, Joseph A., Jr., *DeHaviland DH-4*, Dayton, Oh.: United States Air Force Museum, 1983; Dayton Wright factory file, USAFM.

SL 6:   Loening 1968, 1973; Renstrom 1975; Solberg 1979. In person interview with Harold Johnson, operator of the Moraine Airpark airport, April 5, 1984.

SL 7:   Foerste 1915; Hallion 1978; Harris 1970; Hooven 1978; Renstrom 1975; Young and Fitzgerald 1983. Telephone interview with Gourley Darroch, owner of the property, July 27, 1984.

SL 8:   Stein 1985; Holder 1983; Dempsey 1984.

SL 9:   Andrews 1975; Fisk 1980; Houser 1977; Kelly 1950; Ronald and Ronald 1983; Wright 1915. Photocopied letters from Asahel Wright to Dan Wright, Jr., 1980 supplement to Andrews 1975, WSU; in person interview with Darryl Kenning, Centerville City Manager, Oct. 5, 1982; in person interview with Mary Aldridge, Centerville Historical Society, Oct. 14, 1982; in person interview with Doris Scott, July 14, 1983.

SL 10:   Ronald and Ronald 1983; Renstrom 1975. Wright Library, "Background Information -- Brief History," mimeo, n.d.

SL 11:   Andrews 1975; Leslie 1983; Miller, Ivonette 1978; Renstrom 1975; Williams 1925; Young and Fitzgerald 1983. *Dayton Daily News* June 7, 1981; "Hawthorn Hill Has a Special Place in World History" and "Hawthorn Hill," NCR Historical Reprints; Dayton newspapers, DL; letter from Lora B. Cleary, Grand Rapids Public Museum, to H. Eugene Kniess, NCR, mimeo, Nov. 2, 1973; mimeographed documents from the United Theological Seminary archives provided by John G. Lepp; personal letter to the author from Frederick I. Kuhns, former student at Moraine Park school, April 23, 1984.

SL 12: Ronald and Ronald 1981. Sikora, Mary, "They're All at Woodland," *The Magazine*, Sept. 4, 1983; U. D. Research Institute, *Advanced Research and Applied Technology*, Dayton, Oh.:University of Dayton Research Institute, n.d.; Woodland Cemetery brochure, n.d.

East Anchor

EA 1:   Air Force Museum Foundation 1980; Anderton 1981; Apple 1983; Ronald and Ronald 1983; Jacobs 1984; Kelly 1950. Shook, Howard and Joseph M. Williams, "The Bomb," *The Magazine*, Sept., 18, 1983; Dayton *Journal Herald*, May 22, 1984; personnel files, USAFM; letter from Shari E. Christy, June 19, 1996.

EA 2:   Angelucci 1973; Hallion 1978; Marcosson 1947; Renstrom 1975; Smith 1939. Newspaper clippings, DL; Wright Memorial Commission Trustees correspondence and records, WSU.

EA 3:   Franklin Institute 1978; Hallion 1978; Kelly 1950; Leslie 1983; Marcosson 1947; Munson 1969; Renstrom 1975: Talbert 1953; Wescott and Degen 1983. Hodgkins, Cleo Wilson, *A Tale of Two Cities*, 2nd ed., Fairborn, Oh.: The Fairborn Area Chamber of Commerce, 1981; Wright Company catalog, WSU; *Wright Brothers Historical Walking Trail* brochure, 1991.

EA 4:   Air Force Magazine 1985; Apple 1983; Renstrom 1975; Tavender 1967. Wright-Patterson Air Force Base, *Heritage Tour* brochure; Wright-Patterson Air Force Base file, USAFM; Wright-Patterson Air Force Base publications from Media Relations, Aeronautical Systems Center.

EA 5:   Angelucci 1973; Nolan and Zamonski 1977. Wright State, *Take A Look*, Dayton, Oh,: Wright State University, 1984; in person interview with Dr. Patrick B. Nolan, Wright State University Archives, Jan. 7, 1983.

North Loop

NL 1:   Casey 1964; Horan 1980; Loening 1968; McKay 1981; Smith 1939; Solberg 1979; Tavender 1967. McCook Field file, Macready and Harris personnel files, USAFM; McCook Field file, WSU; *Dayton Daily News* Feb. 27, 1983.

NL 2:   Glassman 1930; Horan 1980; Murphy 1930; Tavender 1967. Harris personnel file, USAFM.

NL 3:   Gunston 1978; Williams 1941 to 1950. Martin, Richard, "Little Robot," no publication name. n.d.; "Roy McGuire Rates Place in Auto Pilot History," *Skyways Flyer*, n.d.; in person interview with Robert Nadolsky, McGuire Products Co. owner, July 6, 1983; *Dayton Daily News* Aug. 15, 1976.

NL 4:   Miller, Irene 1982. Telephone interview with Mrs. Ben Moser, June 30, 1983; in person interview with Don Reed, former vice president of International Flare, Sept. 1, 1983,

NL 5:   Brandly 1979; Tavender 1967. Waco file, WSU; *Troy Daily News* articles, Troy Historical Society; personal letter to the author from Ray Brandly, National Waco Club, May 30,1983; telephone interview with Harold Johnson, June 19, 1996.

NL 6:   *THE WACO WORD.* Vol. 17, No. 1.

NL 7:   Angelucci 1973; Brandly 1979; Juptner 1962; Taylor 1969; Jeager and Rutan 1987. Hartzell, *The Story of Hartzell Walnut Propellers*, Piqua, Oh.: Hartzell, n.d.; Hartzell, *A Century of Progress*, Piqua, Oh.: Hartzell, 1975; in person interview with Jim Reedy, TRW Hartzell, June 17, 1982; letter to the author from Arthur R. Disbrow, June 27, 1996.

NL 8:   Gunston 1978; Williams 1935 to 1941. Deardorf, Barb, "Home of Flight, Home for McCauley," *Dayton USA*, December 1978; Dussault, John, "A Brief History of McCauley," mimeo, 1981; *Dayton Daily News* April 19, 1992, August 26, 1992, August 27, 1993.

NL 9:   Air Force Museum Foundation 1980; Beringer 1955; General Motors 1960; Gunston 1978; Roberts 1978. Aeroproducts Div., *Blades for Victory: The Story of the Aeroproducts Propeller and the Men and Women Who Built It*, Vandalia, Oh.: Aeroproducts Div., General Motors Corp., 1944.

NL 10:   Boesen 1971,1974; Glassman 1930; Beals n.d. Polk, R. L. & Co., *Polks Piqua (Miami County, Ohio) City Directory*, Columbus, Oh.: R. L. Polk & Co., Publishers, 1941 to 1955; Lear personnel file, USAFM; telephone interview with Al Butterfield, employee of former building occupant, Aug. 16, 1983; telephone interview with Mrs. Leon Wise, current building occupant, Aug, 16, 1983.

NL 11:   Beringer 1929; Conover 1932; Juptner 1962; Williams 1926 to 1928. Dayton Dept. of Aviation, "City of Dayton, Department of Aviation" and "The Workplace of Aviation," mimeos, n.d.; newspaper clippings, DL; in person interview with Charles L. Fister, Dayton airport, July 14, 1983; telephone interview with Roy Williams, July 5, 1996.

NL 12:   Jackson 1980; Wolters 1979. Dayton *Journal Herald* Sept. 29, 1984; Rasor journal and newspaper clippings, Brookville Museum; in person interview with Mrs. Herbert Rasor, July 16, 1983.

REFERENCES

Air Force Magazine. "Guide to USAF Bases at Home and Abroad." *Air Force Magazine* 68 (May 1985).

Air Force Museum Foundation. *United States Air Force Museum*. Wright-Patterson AFB, Oh.: Air Force Museum Foundation, Inc., 1980.

Anderton, David A. *The History of the U. S Air Force*. New York: Cresent Books, 1981.

Andrews, Alfred S. *The Andrews, Clapp, Stokes, Wright, Van Cleve Genealogies*, rev. ed. Fort Lauderdale, Fla.: Alfred S. Andrews, 1975.

Angelucci, Enzo. *Airplanes: From the Dawn of Flight to the Present Day*. New York: McGraw-Hill Book Company, 1973.

Apple, Nick P. and Gene Gurney. *The Air Force Museum*. 4th rev. ed. New York: Crown Publishers, Inc. 1983.

Ball, Fred S. "The Genesis of Maxwell Field at Montgomery, Alabama," 1929. Copy of published article from author's grandson, Richard A. Ball, Jr.

Beals, Timothy J. *A History of the SLC Avionic Systems Corp. 1930-1987*. Smith Industries, n.d.

Beringer, Sarah M. *The Beginning and Future of Aviation*. Dayton, Oh.: Sarah M. Beringer, 1929.

_____. *History of Dayton Industries*. Dayton, Oh.: Sarah M. Beringer, 1955.

Boesen, Victor. *They Said It Couldn't Be Done: The Incredible Story of Bill Lear*. Garden City N.Y.: Doubleday & Co., Inc. 1971.

_____ *William P. Lear: From High School Dropout to Space Age Inventor*. New York: Hawthorn Books, 1974.

Boyd, Thomas A. *Professional Amateur: The Biography of Charles Franklin Kettering*. New York: E. P Dutton & Co., Inc., 1957.

Brandly, Raymond H. *Waco Airplanes: "Ask Any Pilot."* Dayton, Oh.: Raymond H. Brandly, 1979.

Bryan, Ashley, comp. *I Greet The Dawn: Poems by Paul Laurence Dunbar*. New York: Atheneum, 1978.

Carillon Park. *Our Antique Autos*. Dayton, Oh.: Carillon Park, 1982.

Casey, Louis S. *The First Nonstop Coast-to-Coast Flight and the Historic T-2 Airplane*. Vol 1, No. 1 of Smithsonian Annals of Flight. Washington, D.C.: Smithsonian Institution, National Air Museum, 1964.

Conover, Charlotte Reeve. *Dayton, Ohio: An Intimate History*. New York: Lewis Historical Publishing Company, Inc., 1932.

Coombs, Charles. *Bicycling*. New York: William Morrow & Co., 1972.

Crowther, Samuel. *John H. Patterson: Pioneer in Industrial Welfare*. Garden City, NY: Doubleday, Page & Co, 1923.

Davenport, William Wyatt. *Gyro! The Life and Times of Lawrence Sperry*. New York: Charles Scribner's Sons, 1978.

Dempsey, Charles A. "A Dream Come True." *The Engineer* (October 1984).

Drury, A. W. *History of the City of Dayton and Montgomery County, Ohio*. Vol 1. Chicago: S. J. Clarke Publishing Company, 1909.

Edison Institute. *Dedication of the Wright Brothers Home and Shop in Greenfield Village*. Dearborn, Mich.: The Edison Institute, 1938.

Faber, C. W., comp. *New Dayton Illustrated: The Gem City through a Camera*. Dayton, Oh.: The National Coupon Publishing Co., 1893.

Fisk, Fred C. "The Wright Brothers' Bicycles." *The Wheelmen* 17 (November 1980).

Foerste, August F. *An Introduction to Geology of the Vicinity of Dayton with Special Reference to Hills and Dales and Moraine Park*. Indianapolis: Hollenbeck Press, 1915.

Franklin Institute. *Conquest of the Skies: The Wright Brothers Portfolio*. Philadelphia: The Franklin Institute, 1978.

General Motors. *Story of General Motors*. Detroit: General Motors Corporation, 1960.

Gibbs-Smith, Charles Harvard. *The World's First Practical Airplane: The Wright Flyer III in Carillon Park, Dayton*. Dayton, Oh.: Carillon Park, 1971.

Glassman, Don. *Jump! Tales of the Caterpillar Club*. New York: Simon and Schuster, Inc., 1930.

Glines, Carroll V. *The Wright Brothers: Pioneers of Power Flight*. New York: Franklin Watts, Inc. 1968.

Gunston, Bill. *Aviation: The Complete Story of Man's Conquest of the Air*. London: Octopus Books Limited, 1978.

Hallion, Richard P., ed. T*he Wright Brothers: Heirs of Prometheus*. Washington, D. C.: National Air and Space Museum, Smithsonian Institution, 1978.

Harris, Sherwood. *The First to Fly: Aviation's Pioneer Days*. New York: Simon and Schuster, 1970.

Hobbs, Leonard S. *The Wright Brothers' Engines and Their Design*. No. 5 of Smithsonian Annals of Flight. Washington, D.C.: Smithsonian Institution Press, 1971.

Holder, William, "How the Wright B was Built," *Air Force Magazine* (September 1983).

Hooven, Frederick J. "The Wright Brothers Flight Control System." *Scientific American* 239 (November 1978).

Horan, Michael. *Parachuting Folklore: Evolution of Freefall*. Richmond, Ind.: Parachuting Resources, 1980.

Houser, Howard R., ed. *A Sense of Place: In Centerville and Washington Township*. Dayton, Oh.: The Centerville Historical Society, 1977.

Hutchinson, Ronald V. "Skylarking: 1917-1918." United States Air Force Museum Research Department, Dayton, Oh. Mimeo, 1943.

International Air Races, Inc. *A Brochure on Aviation and the City of Dayton: An Official Souvenir Program, International Air Races*. Dayton, Oh: International Air Races, Inc., 1924.

Jackson, Donald Dale, ed. *The Aeronauts*. Alexandria, Va.: Time-Life Books, 1980.

Jacobs, James W. *Enshrinee Album: The First Twenty-One Years*. Dayton, Oh: National Aviation Hall of Fame, 1984.

Junior League of Dayton, Ohio, Inc. *Dayton: A History in Photographs*, 2nd ed. Dayton, Oh.: The Junior League of Dayton, Inc., 1982.

Juptner, Joseph P. *U. S. Civil Aircraft*. Vol. 1. Los Angeles: Aero Publishers, Inc., 1962.

Kelly, Fred C. *The Wright Brothers: A Biography Authorized by Orville Wright*. New York: Ballantine Books, 1950.

Landmark Committee. *Landmark Committee of Montgomery County, Ohio Report.* Dayton, Oh.: Landmark Committee, 1968.

Leslie, Stuart W. *Boss Kettering.* New York: Columbia University Press, 1983.

Loening, Grover. *Takeoff into Greatness: How American Aviation Grew so Big so Fast.* New York: G. P. Putnam's Sons, 1968.

_____ *Amphibian: The Story of the Loening Biplane.* Greenwich, Conn.: New York Graphic Society, 1973.

Loeper, John L. *Away We Go!: On Bicycles in 1898.* New York: Atheneum, 1982.

Marcosson, Isaac F. *Colonel Deeds: Industrial Builder.* New York: Dodd, Mead & Company, 1947.

Maxwell Air Force Base. "Maxwell Air Force Base History: 1910-1939." Maxwell Air Force Base, Montgomery, Ala. Mimeo, n.d.

McKay, Ernest A. *A World To Conquer: The Epic Story of the First Around-the-World Flight.* New York: Arco Publishing, Inc., 1981.

Miller, Irene E., ed. *A History of Miami County, Ohio*, rev. ed. Tipp City, Oh.: The Miami County Historical Society, 1982.

Miller, Ivonette Wright. *Wright Reminiscences.* Dayton, Oh.: Ivonette Wright Miller, 1978.

Morgan, Arthur E. *The Miami Conservancy District.* New York: McGraw-Hill Book Company, 1951.

Munson, Kenneth. *Pioneer Aircraft, 1903-1914: The Pocket Encyclopedia of World Aircraft in Color.* New York: The Macmillan Co., 1969.

Murphy, Charles J. V. *Parachute.* New York: G. P. Putnam's Sons, 1930.

Nolan, Patrick B. and John A. Zamonski. *The Wright Brothers Collection: A Guide to the Technical, Business and Legal, Genealogical, Photographic, and other Archives at Wright State University.* New York: Garland Publishing, Inc. 1977.

Purcell, Thomas F. *Bicycles on Parade: A Brief History.* Minneapolis: Lerner Publications Company, 1980.

Renstrom, Arthur G. *Wilbur and Orville Wright: A Chronology Commemorating the Hundredth Anniversary of the Birth of Orville Wright August 19, 1971.* Washington, D.C.: Library of Congress, 1975.

_____ *Wilbur and Orville Wright: Pictorial Materials.* Washington, D.C.: Library of Congress, 1982.

Roberts, Carl. *200 Years of Progress: A History of Dayton and the Miami Valley.* Dubuque, Ia.: Kendall/Hunt Publishing Co., 1978.

Rolfe, Douglas. *Airplanes of the World: 1490 to 1969*, rev. and enl. New York: Simon and Schuster, 1969.

Ronald, Bruce and Virginia Ronald. *Dayton: The Gem City.* Tulsa, Okla.: Continental Heritage Press, Inc., 1981.

_____ *Oakwood: The Far Hills.* Dayton, Oh.: Reflections Press, 1983.

Smith, George B. "Common Clay: An Autobiography." Mimeo, 1939.

Solberg, Carl. *Conquest of the Skies: A History of Commercial Aviation in America.* Boston: Little, Brown & Co., 1979.

Stein, E. P. *Flight of the Vin Fiz.* New York: Arbor House, 1985.

Talbert, Ansel E. *Famous Airports of the World.* New York: Random House, 1953.

Tavender, Bert, ed. *1917-1967 50th Anniversary: A Pictorial Review.* Riverside, Cal.: Armed Services Publishers, 1967.

Taylor, John W. R., ed. *Milestones of the Air: Jane's 100 Significant Aircraft.* New York: McGraw-Hill Book Co., 1969.

Taylor, Michael J. H. and David Monday. *Milestones of Flight.* London: Jane's Publishing Company, Limited, 1983.

Wagner, Ray. *American Combat Planes*, 3rd ed. Garden City, N.Y.: Doubleday & Company, 1982.

Weaver, Margaret. "The Wright Brothers at 22 South Williams Street: 1895 to 1897." Mimeo, 1983.

Wescott, Lyanne and Paula Degen. *Wind and Sand: The Story of the Wright Brothers at Kitty Hawk.* New York: Harry N. Abrams, Inc., Publishers, 1983.

Whitehouse, Arch. *The Military Airplane: Its History and Development.* Garden City, N.Y.: Doubleday & Company, Inc., 1971.

Williams, C. S. *Williams' Dayton Directory.* Cincinnati, Oh.: C. S. Williams, Publisher, 1856-57 and on.

Wolters, Richard A. *The World of Silent Flight.* New York: McGraw-Hill Book Co., 1979.

Wright, Curtis. *Genealogical and Biological Notices of the Descendants of Sir John Wright of Kelvedon Hall, Essex, England, in England and America.* Carthage, Mo.: Curtis Wright, 1915.

Yeager, Jeana and Dick Rutan with Phil Patton. *Voyager.* New York: Alfred A. Knopf, Inc., 1987.

Young, Rosamond McPherson. *Boss Kett: A Life of Charles F. Kettering.* New York: David McKay Company, Inc., 1961.

Young, Rosamond and Catharine Fitzgerald. *Twelve Seconds to the Moon: A Story of the Wright Brothers.* 2nd ed. Dayton, Oh: United States Air Force Museum Foundation, Inc., 1983.

INDEX

ABOUT THE AUTHOR

Mary Ann Johnson is a native of Dayton, Ohio who became interested in researching local aviation history as a member of the Board of Trustees of Aviation Trail, Inc. Now retired, she has worked as an economic planner for the Miami Valley Regional Planning Commission, as a parttime instructor in economics at Sinclair Community College, in Dayton, and for a number of survey research organizations. She has a B. A. in sociology from Miami University, Oxford, Ohio, and a M. S. in economics from Wright State University, Dayton. Mary Ann and her husband, Rich, are the parents of four grown children.

AVIATION TRAIL LOG

SITE	DATE OF VISIT	COMMENTS